SHEFFIELD HALLAM UNIVERSITY
LEARNING & IT SERVICES
ADSETTS CENTRE CITY CAMPUS
SHEFFIELD S1 1WB

101 988 357 X

KT-197-815

ONE WEEK LOAN

Advance copy. First published in Great Britain in 2010.

Copyright © David Jamilly and Tammy Cohen

All rights reserved. No part of this publication may be
reproduced, stored in a retrieval system, or transmitted,
in any form or by any means without the prior written
permission of the publisher, nor be otherwise circulated
in any form of binding or cover other than that in which
it is published and without a similar condition being
imposed on the subsequent purchaser.

ISBN: 978-1-907499-77-7

Indepenpress Publishing
25 Eastern Place, Brighton BN2 1GJ

Cover Design: Arati Devasher

Interior pages designed and typeset
in Adobe Caslon Pro by Arati Devasher
www.aratidevasher.com

Printed and bound in Great Britain
by Thomson Litho Ltd

FSC
Mixed Sources
Product group from well-managed
forests and other controlled sources
Cert no. TT-COC-002366
www.fsc.org
© 1996 Forest Stewardship Council

On production of a £20 receipt from any
registered charity, another copy of this book is
available free of charge from the publisher.

Sheffield Hallam University
Learning and Information Services
WITHDRAWN FROM STOCK

Secret Millionaire
David Jamilly's

party
peple

how we make
million$
from having fun

David Jamilly & Tammy Cohen

CONTENTS

FOREWORD

Working in the exciting, ever changing world of parties isn't a job, it's a lifestyle, and I never stop feeling privileged to be part of it. Filming for Channel Four's Secret Millionaire programme, which involved spending eight days living on the breadline, brought home to me just how lucky I am, not only to do the most ideal job in the world, but also to have made a big success of it. It seems incredible that my sister, Kim, and I started Theme Traders back in 1990, and have been throwing parties for the great and good (and some not so good!) ever since. We've learned a fantastic amount over that time, about business and parties and ourselves and it's a real buzz to be able to pass on some of that knowledge in this book. Special thanks to all our team and clients and suppliers, many of whom have remained friends over the years and made the whole experience a real joy.

Throwing parties for some of the biggest celebrity names around has been a privilege – and an eye opener! While client confidentiality precludes us naming individuals (some names in this account have been changed), it's fair to say we've seen and done an awful lot over the years, but the incredible thing is we're still learning all the time.

As with any business, we've had some hilarious challenges and been taught some tough lessons, but we've also staged some completely magical events that will live in the memories of those present for their entire lives – and I'm incredibly proud of that.

David Jamilly

David was hiding in the toilet.

It's fair to say that the Formula 1 party, being filmed for Sky TV (then still in its infancy), had not gone to plan.

A slight miscalculation with the dry ice machine and the power sockets had meant the guests, among them a fair smattering of big-name celebrities, had narrowly escaped being electrocuted on their way in. David and his sister Kim, who'd organised the event, had envisaged a dramatic entrance, where awestruck party-goers would drift down a black-out tunnel, lit only with the dimmest of low-level lighting and atmospheric dry ice rising up eerily from the ground. Instead, the dry ice machine had leaked in a gloopy puddle all over the floor, and the low-level lighting, which had all been plugged in through the same socket (dangerously close to the rising puddle of water) had shorted, leaving the guests to pick their way gingerly through the murky, slightly damp-smelling darkness, down a partially-flooded passageway.

Inside the venue, things had gone from bad to a whole lot worse. Guests were seated at tables, in full view of the stage above which towered the party's pièce-de-résistance; a massive wall of balloons, twenty feet high, spelling out the words 'Nigel Mansell World Champion'. Though no one was aware of it yet, behind the front layer of balloons was a second wall, which would be spectacularly revealed when the first surface was detonated in a controlled explosion later in the evening. Everything had been designed for maximum dramatic impact.

What no one could have predicted, was that owing to the heat of the lights in the vast function room, the glue holding the letters to the balloons would start melting. Over the course of the meal, one by one, the letters slid off. At first few people noticed, but after a while all eyes were turned towards the balloon display as guests tried to guess which one would be next. By the time coffee was served, the message puzzlingly read 'i sell ham', and half the diners were too convulsed with laughter to do justice to their petits fours.

After the dinnertime disaster, David could hardly wait for the speeches and awards to start so that the guests' attention would be drawn away from the balloons and onto the stage itself where the great and the good of British motor racing had gathered to pay tribute to Nigel Mansell, one time Formula 1 World Champion. David watched with mounting excitement from backstage, aware – as the audience were not – of the imminent explosion, which had been timed to coincide with Nigel Mansell's appearance on the stage, and which would blow the first wall of balloons sky high. He was sure the guests would be so bowled over by the drama and surprise of the explosion that they'd forget all about the fiasco of the waterlogged tunnel and the moulting balloons.

The blast, when it came, was just as spectacular as they'd hoped for. But there was one little problem. The metal scaffolding, which had been holding the wall of balloons in place, was destabilised by the explosion and began to wobble, at first imperceptibly and then, as David watched with mounting horror, with growing momentum. It was clearly about to topple over. The question was, which way would it fall? On the stage, blissfully unaware of the unfolding drama and alarmingly close to the precarious rigging's trajectory, were racing driver Jackie Stewart and a wheelchair-bound Frank Williams. For what could only have been a split-second but which felt like a lifetime, David fought back nausea as the metal scaffolding continued to wobble behind the Formula 1 boss's head, before finally crashing to the ground – mercifully well away from the stage.

That was the moment he made a dash for the toilets, unable to face the inevitable recriminations. He and Kim and their fledgling company, Theme Traders, had been on such a high in recent months, turning out successful event after successful event. It was as if everything they did turned to gold. When they'd been asked to arrange this party, it was long before the days when a raft of experts would be on hand to calculate the effects of any given explosion. David hadn't even entertained the possibility of anything going wrong. Everything they'd done up until this point had been an unmitigated triumph. He simply couldn't believe what had just happened.

Outside the toilet cubicle he could hear someone calling his name, the oh-too-familiar voice growing nearer and nearer. The client was looking for him. Slumping miserably against the door, David agonised about what he would say to his sister and co-partner Kim. How would he break it to her that the party they'd planned out so self-confidently had been a disaster, and the company was in all likelihood finished?

Meanwhile, the footsteps were drawing closer. There was nothing else for it. It was time to face the music.

Reluctantly unlocking the door, David sidled outside, too mortified even to meet the other man's eyes.

"Well," the client began sternly and David steeled himself for the attack, "I think that went off very well, don't you?"

One thing he should have learned by now about parties – never, ever try to second guess the client.

David felt weak with relief. The guests had thought the crackling noise from the electrical sockets in the entrance tunnel was part of the intended effect! Diners had found the misspelt balloons hysterical! Frank Williams hadn't been decapitated! Theme Traders, the event management business he and Kim had set up from scratch, would live to party another day!

But as he helped cleared away the wreckage of the party – the shrivelled remnants of popped balloons, the mangled metal rigging, David couldn't help wondering, not for the first time, whether there might be easier ways to make a living and, more importantly, just how on earth he and Kim had ended up here…

all in the genes

Grandpa David and his travelling cinema

Every story has to start somewhere.

To understand how Kim and David Jamilly, a headstrong, non-conformist brother and sister from North London, came to be hiding in toilets and running one of the most successful events companies in Europe, you have to go right back to the late 1890s and the Middle East where David Jamilly (the first!), their paternal grandfather, had spotted an entrepreneurial opportunity – travelling cinema.

Armed with his projector and marquee, David left his native Baghdad and criss-crossed Saudi Arabia, journeying further to Singapore and India, bringing his magical machine to people who'd never otherwise have witnessed the wonders of moving pictures.

He'd arrive in a prosperous town or a village and immediately advertise his show with posters and a parade to let people know what was happening. Then he'd set up his tent and wait for the punters to flood in.

Of course, it didn't always go exactly the way he'd hoped. Don't forget, this was before the days of mainstream cinema. Many times, people would react with horror at the sight of moving images on a screen and run screaming from the tent. The sight of a paying audience fleeing for the hills isn't one that a budding entrepreneur welcomes but David didn't give up. He knew that cinema wasn't going to be a mere passing trend and he wanted to be in on it from the start. His perseverance provided some valuable lessons about business:

3 things David Jamilly (the first) learned about business:

- Identify a demand, and supply it.
- Promote your service (of course, not everyone has elephants and snake charmers at hand, ready to parade through the streets, but make use of whatever resources you have).
- Don't be afraid to put your faith into something new – be at the head of a trend or a movement, not chasing the tail end.

David Jamilly made a lot of money with his travelling cinema and, now a wealthy man, decided to come to England. Possibly his decision was prompted by a wise chief in one of the villages he visited who watched the people moving around on screen with interest, but without the usual awe, and who afterwards remarked prophetically, "True, this is magic – but one day they will *speak.*" (Also proving that true visionaries can be found in the most unlikely places.) It was the start of a new century; cinema was about to take off in the UK, and David once again wanted to be in at the forefront. He opened what became a very successful cinema in Harlesden, heralding the event with a parade down the high street (with the local Boys Brigade filling in for the elephants this time).

In around 1910, he turned his hand to film distribution, setting up several offices around D'Arblay St in Soho. The company flourished. Jamilly bought himself a country estate in Rudgwick, Surrey, although he never lived there. He also found himself an English wife, Lydia, and had three very English sons, Victor, Edward and Joe.

3 more things David Jamilly (the first) learned about business:

- Think Big. Going from one man and his tent, to film distribution empire takes vision.
- Diversify. If you stick to the first thing you make a success of, you risk becoming outdated, or being overtaken by the opposition.
- Expand. When one office gets too busy, don't turn business away, get another one.

As the 20th century staggered through one war and on inexorably towards the next, David Jamilly, first generation immigrant, business tycoon, family man, continued to thrive. He was one of the original members of the Cinema Veterans

Society, he met Charlie Chaplin, he wrote for the influential *The Kinematograph and Lantern Weekly* magazine and two of his three sons attended the prestigious Highgate boys' school. In fact, during the Second World War, he even offered to loan out the estate in Rudgwick when the school was threatened with evacuation. He became, in short, a pillar of the society he'd gatecrashed just a few short decades before.

But then David made one fundamental, crucial error. He became complacent. In the face of a world which was changing faster than the weather, he stopped diversifying and stuck to what he knew. He'd been riding the wave of the zeitgeist for his entire adult life, but now he foolhardily abandoned his board

David:

"Successful entrepreneurs have to keep changing – otherwise they'll become defunct. Theme Traders is constantly adapting. When everyone else was concentrating on party planning, we built up the props side of our business. Now the props industry is saturated, we're looking towards the luxury and B2B markets. We have to keep moving and we have to stay one step ahead of the rest."

and trod water instead. Having made his name in a field of ever-evolving technology, he stopped evolving with it. When David (the first) died in the late 1940s, he was still a wealthy man, but the writing was on the wall for the cinema empire he'd built up. Within a few years of his death, the estate in Rudgwick was sold as were the offices in Soho, piled with dusty old films made from materials so toxic they were wont to explode on touch.

Which is how David (the second) and Kim, who weren't even born at the time their paternal grandfather died, came to learn early on in life the most basic principle of business:

Always adapt to keep pace with a changing market.

Victor Jamilly and his very good idea

David Jamilly (the first), as we've heard, had three sons of whom Victor was the middle. One day Victor went into a coffee shop in Swiss Cottage for a hot chocolate and a scone and came out with a wife, having fallen in love with the waitress whose name was Audrey. The couple went on to have three children who grew up with their paternal grandmother, Lydia, in Golders Green, North London – David (the second), Kim and younger brother Jonathan.

Though his children grew up relishing their free trips to the pictures, courtesy of Grandma Lydia who had a free cinema pass for eternity, Victor wasn't about to follow his father into the film business, which he could see was already ailing in Britain. Neither was he about to follow older brother Edward into an established profession. Instead, he and his friend Laurence Krieger set about creating a number of small businesses – record shops, milk bars and, on one misguided occasion, a launderette (why did no one explain that colours and whites fare better in a separate wash?). Wherever they spotted an opportunity, they took it.

One day in the 1950s, the two young men wandered into an auction room in the West End where supplies of defunct Red Cross stock left over from the war were being auctioned off. Figuring they had little to lose, they bought up the stock and, to their surprise, managed to sell it on without much problem, so of course they bought some more... and more... Eventually Victor realised they were onto a good thing and opened a shop on a prominent corner near London's Euston Square Station selling army surplus supplies. The shop was called Laurence Corner and went on to become one of the most iconic cult fashion institutions of late 20th century London.

In the beginning though, it was just a musty-smelling, 5-storey shop, full of piles of old stuff left over from the war that nobody else seemed to want. Great coats, khaki combat trousers, sailor tops, gas masks, you name it, Victor Jamilly would try to flog it. Both David (the younger) and Kim would come at weekends and play among the dusty boxes of funny-looking clothes and hats, Zulu warrior shields and even musical instruments – drums and trumpets which had somehow survived the heavy duty wear and tear of military band life.

"I'm going to work here when I leave school," said the young David.

"Nonsense," his father smiled indulgently. David, after all, was a born academic, gliding effortlessly through exam after exam. He was clearly going to go on to be a professional of some hazy description.

"I'm going to work here too," said the young Kim.

What Victor Jamilly did right:

- Spot an opportunity.
- Spot another when the first didn't work out... and then another...
- Start small and grow with his market.

"I don't think so," came the jocular paternal response. Kim was already showing herself to be a feisty, unconventional girl who didn't take kindly to authority. The thought of her working in this rather stuffy atmosphere alongside all these fusty old relics was hard to imagine.

David and Kim Jamilly were clearly destined for far bigger and better things than a jumped-up junk shop. If Victor Jamilly could have known that his son and daughter would each notch up nearly two decades apiece working amid the boxes and the dust he'd have eaten his genuine Russian army hat (with flaps). During that time Laurence Corner became one of the most talked about fashion emporiums in the country, attracting everyone from Michael Jackson to Mick Jagger and providing inspiration for cultural trends ranging from the Adam Ant albums to the Indiana Jones movies.

As the 1960s swung into life all around him, all Victor knew was that there was a market for stuff the army didn't want any more, and that after the austerity of the war years, fashion was becoming frivolous again, ironic and irreverent. And somehow he'd found himself – just as his father before him – in at the beginning.

Insider tip: how to throw an unforgettable launch party

When Grandpa David was parading elephants down dusty village streets proclaiming the arrival of his travelling cinema, or sending Boys Brigades marching through Harlesden's busy centre, he had clearly grasped the value of advance promotion and, in particular, the effect of a grand opening. A century later, his grandchildren would hone the launch party to an exact science. Here's how to do it in style:

How to throw an unforgettable launch party

- Take time to tailor the event to the product or service you're launching. Hunt around for a venue that sends out the right messages.
- Think carefully about the guest list. You want to have enough people to spread the word, but keep it selective enough to create a buzz (and prevent costs from spiralling)
- Make sure the invitations are attention-grabbing; this will attract the right number (and calibre) of people as this will be their first insight into both your product and the event itself.
- If you're inviting the press, do your research; make sure you choose publications that fit with the image and target market of the enterprise you're launching and…
- … be specific about whether or not they're allowed to bring guests.

CHAPTER TWO
the latent entrepreneurs

There's a commonly held myth, which says that entrepreneurs are born not made; similarly that all budding entrepreneurs are programmed from infancy to sell contraband to classmates from their satchels or make millions from their bedrooms, when they should be doing their homework. They just can't help themselves from doing business, goes the myth. Well, Kim and David Jamilly are living proof that sometimes the exact opposite holds true.

Growing up, the brother and sister had just one business in mind – the business of having fun. The house in London's leafy Hampstead Garden Suburb, where the Jamillys moved after Golders Green, was a hub of activity, with neighbourhood children coming and going, music playing and lots and lots of parties.

At first it was children's parties with entertainers and magicians and adults getting gently sozzled in the background, but as they grew older, the parties grew more anarchic. There are certain advantages to the 'older brother, younger sister' dynamic, particularly when it comes to mixing 'n' matching your mates. David's friends and Kim's friends would pair off to various bedrooms and snog under piles of coats, or David's band of the moment would set up on the landing and hold court to enthralled (or intoxicated) guests.

But it took a mutual friend of both Kim and David's, the colourfully named Pinball Geoff (incidentally now one of the world's leading experts on pinball) who lived round the corner, to take the Jamilly's party-giving onto dizzying new heights of sophistication.

3 Things Pinball Geoff taught the young Jamillys about throwing a party:

- Pay attention to mood. Geoff was the first person Kim and David knew who realised that swapping a normal light bulb for a red one completely altered the ambience – even of a sweaty teenage bedroom.
- The importance of transformation. Sticking painted egg box cartons to the bedroom walls may not have been the pinnacle of chic, but it served a crucial party function – that of transforming an everyday space into something special, of creating a different state.
- The existence of the 'wow factor'. Egg boxes, red light bulbs… separately they don't amount to much but together they were enough to make a bunch of 1970s 15-year-olds hesitate for a minute at the doorway and go 'wow'. That 'wow' factor is still the cornerstone of David and Kim's party philosophy. Thanks Geoff.

Party piece: David's ultimate transformation party

The guests arrive at an anonymous entrance and are ushered down dark corridors into a completely white room, with a single bare bulb hanging from the middle of the ceiling. There is nothing else, just this stark white cube with its dangling naked bulb. When they are all gathered inside, puzzled, slightly apprehensive, and asking each other what on earth is going on, the walls of the cube suddenly drop away, to reveal that they are actually inside a grand, awe-inspiring venue like a museum or an art gallery. That process of transformation and revelation creates a heightened state of anticipation in party guests, a suspension of disbelief, particularly if it's unexpected.

Naturally the parties they attended weren't just home-grown affairs – all over London friends or friends of friends were throwing, or knew of someone who was throwing, a bash. And wherever there was a bash going on, the Jamillys could be found. David lost track of the number of times he and a friend staggered out of a party only to stand shivering in a phone box waiting for morning, after telling their parents they were sleeping over at each other's houses.

But while the Jamilly siblings were very accomplished at enjoying their leisure time, school was a different story. David, who excelled academically, nevertheless found the structures and hierarchies of English public school life oppressive. He wasn't one of the rugby lads, didn't get along with the boys-own culture and HATED still having to wear shorts at the age of twelve. This was the era of Carnaby Street and Kensington Market, of Woodstock and fashion expressionism. It was not the era of grey flannel shorts.

"I'll tell you what," his father told him, "if you get ten O Levels, I'll let you leave school."

For Victor Jamilly it must have seemed like a safe bet. Few people at that time took more than eight O Levels. And besides, if someone was going to actually pass all those exams, wouldn't they decide it would be a waste not to stay on at school and take A Levels?

David duly sailed through ten O Levels. Within a month of getting his results, he was working for his father at Laurence Corner.

Kim's problems with school came in a different form. She just couldn't abide being told what to do. "She's disruptive," the teachers told Victor. "She has a problem with authority." "Her skirts are too short."

At the age of fifteen years and two months, Kim left school and before she was sixteen, she too was working at Laurence Corner. It would be the duo's home from home for the best part of twenty years.

When David first started working in the higgledy-piggledy, multi-storeyed shop on the corner of Hampstead Road, it had yet to become a haunt of the famous and stylish. Instead it was mostly utilitarian, selling fisherman's trousers to... well, fishermen. The shop's basement and darkest corners (of which there were many) were full of unexpected oddities bought by Victor on a whim – two thousand egg cups, fifty thousand hymn books. But little by little, word began to spread that here was a treasure trove of quirky, individual and, above all, affordable fashion – don't forget this was forty years pre-Primark.

By the time Kim came to join the staff, Laurence Corner was becoming one of the hippest places to hang out. Its topography, its geography, its idiosyncratic contents, its laid back staff, the tantalising possibility of browsing next to one of its celebrity clientele, conspired to make it one of the coolest shopping experiences in London.

Time and again, as 60s and then 70s fashion kicked against the conventionality and austerity of post-war Britain, army surplus was at the forefront of the season's trends – sailor shirts, great coats, jodhpurs were mixed irreverently with frills and flowers, long hair and beards. Jacqueline Bisset set male hearts thumping by posing in a Laurence Corner string vest and very little else; the Beatles reportedly gained the inspiration for the costumes on the Sergeant Peppers Lonely Hearts Club Band record cover from Laurence Corner's stock of Edwardian dress uniforms; Keith Moon nearly caused a riot when he browsed through the store and a young, heavily made up Boy George used to hang hopefully around the hats and rubber suit displays.

So did David begrudge his little sister coming in just as things started to take off, having put in his apprenticeship in the stuffy gentleman's outfitters' atmosphere of the old Laurence Corner?

"Not at all," he insists. Not because the two got on so harmoniously – in fact they argued all the time; not because they had a vision for how the shop could be developed – in fact neither had over-much ambition in that direction; but because Kim was family, and family stuck together.

Besides, Kim was dispatched to work at the new boutique section round the corner from the main shop, so the brother and sister didn't actually physically work together, further minimising the risk of a family rift.

Jane Wormleighton (childhood friend):

"The balance between David and Kim is very interesting – where she is outspoken, David is understated. When David was working at the main Laurence Corner shop and Kim was in the boutique, they established a dynamic and an immediacy of working together that has carried them all the way through."

After work, the altogether more serious business of leisure would begin. Kim had met and married her husband Michel, an easy-going, Hatton Garden diamond dealer, who would be her constant support (often literally) over the years to come, and her free time was largely wrapped up in him. David, however, was intent on taking full advantage of the cultural experiences London had to offer. He had been heavily involved in theatre since school days and played in several bands, one of which even appeared on Top of the Pops. He loved going out to watch the big performers of the time, such as the Who and the Stones, particularly at the groundbreaking Roundhouse venue in Chalk Farm. Their shows were a spectacle in themselves. These weren't bands merely playing through their greatest hits – these performances offered a complete sensory experience, special effects, lighting, costumes props, all working in tandem with the music itself. Although he didn't realise it, David was picking up invaluable tips for his future party business:

- the importance of theatre.
- the need to create an alternate reality, vastly different from the real world.
- there's nothing quite like hearing an audience say 'wow'.

If David Jamilly (the first) had ridden the zeitgeist with his faith in the future of cinema, Victor found himself quite accidentally, right at its epicentre. Three major fashion trends of the time – sailor jackets, military greatcoats, khaki – all seemed to have been created with Laurence Corner in mind.

And the shop's clientele read like a Who's Who of the showbusiness elite of the time. A short while after seeing the Rolling Stones play in Hyde Park, David was mildly surprised to see Mick Jagger come strolling through the doorway. Paul and Linda McCartney were also regular visitors.

On one occasion, a small huddle of people swept in, none of whom David paid much attention to (in truth David rarely recognised any of the famous names who came through the door) until a man sidled up to him:

"Mr Jackson would like the hat," he said, pointing to a pith helmet which was displayed on the wall.

David frowned.

"I'm afraid we don't sell things from the wall display," he said.

The man looked dumbfounded. Then he tried again.

"Mr Jackson would like that helmet."

"But it's from the wall. We don't sell things from the wall."

The man stared at David open-mouthed. Then he said,

"Would it help if I got Mr Jackson to come over and shake hands?"

Before David could reply, he'd disappeared and returned shortly after with his boss, a man even David couldn't fail to recognise. The two men shook hands, Michael Jackson got his helmet and for a while the wall display, which often remained untouched for years on end, had a conspicuous gap.

Meanwhile Kim, who had virtually free rein of the boutique side of Laurence Corner, was discovering a new and hitherto untapped market – fancy dress.

By its very nature, the shop had always had some quirky, fantastical merchandise – heavy red guards' jackets and hats, full nurses' uniforms and of course, the gas masks and diving suits previously worn by submarine workers, which always attracted a very different type of customer.

The fantastical element is what drew so many fashion designers to Laurence Corner, where they'd find inspiration rifling through the stacks of army issue clothing from all over the world. As the anything-goes 70s gave way to the style-conscious 80s, Katherine Hamnett, Zandra Rhodes, Jeff Banks and Vivienne Westwood all made regular pilgrimages to the rambling shop near Euston Square.

People had long come into the shop looking for one-off outfits for special events or fancy dress parties. One day a man came in not wanting to buy a costume, but hire it for a night.

"We don't do that," Kim told him brusquely.

"Why?" asked the man.

"We just don't."

"Why?" asked Kim's husband Michel, when she recounted the scene later.

"We just don't, okay?"

It was not okay. It didn't take a genius to work out that you could make more money hiring something out repeatedly than selling it once.

Michel prevailed; Laurence Corner started hiring out fancy dress costumes, with great success, and Kim realised two fundamental things:

- her husband was sometimes right and
- people will pay a big premium for fantasy – even if it's a never-to-be-repeated fantasy (*especially* if it's a never-to-be-repeated fantasy).

Things to remember when throwing a fancy dress party (part one):

- Keep it simple. Unless you have unlimited access to a theatrical costumiers, steer clear of themes like 'Louis XIV France'. Stick to more general ones, that people can put together easily from things they already have at home.
- Colour-schemes make a safe but effective fancy dress choice. Having everyone dress in purple or in neon or glitter or spots adds an extra level to the experience, as well as a quirky visual dimension. It is also practical and relatively hassle-free.
- Know your guests. If they're adventurous, go for an imaginative fancy dress theme. For the more conservative guestlist, choose a lower-risk option.
- Part of the joy of fancy dress is the opportunity it offers for transformation, freeing guests up to become someone else, at least temporarily. A wig party provides maximum transformation potential

for minimum investment (either of time, money or courage!)

- Have conviction. Once you've decided on a fancy dress theme, make sure you flag it up on the invitations and don't give the impression it's optional. If people think there's a danger they'll be the only ones in costume, chances are they just won't bother.

Incorporating fancy dress into the Laurence Corner repertoire opened up a whole new set of doors. Now the boutique wasn't just about fashion, but about theatre and, more portentously, about parties. The shop introduced a few props into their stock as well as costumes – and Kim was regularly asked round to customer's houses to install the props herself in advance of some event or other. Which, being the kind of girl who liked a challenge, she duly did. Then one day, she got a call from a man called Richard who worked in television and had become a regular in the shop. He wanted to know if she'd be willing to come round to a posh London Hotel and 'dress' a room, in preparation for a television interview being held there.

Kim had never decorated a room in her life, but it just wasn't in her nature to say 'no' (which would later prove a cause for some regret when she accepted a random invitation to act as a painter and decorator – issued by someone who'd found Laurence Corner in the Yellow Pages and got the wrong end of the stick). Arriving at a beautiful hotel in the heart of London, she was shown the room in question, with its stark pillars that couldn't help but reflect TV lights and flashbulbs. She'd been given some black fabric to do the job, but realised instinctively that this would make the room more like a funeral parlour than an atmospheric set so, in a flash of inspiration, she took down some brocade curtains hidden behind a screen at the back of the room and swathed them around the pillars, creating a dramatic, but also intimate effect. Once again, it was the magic of Transformation – something that would later become one of the cornerstones of Kim and David's party planning business. The client was delighted, but despite this success, Kim thought of it as a one-off. Her place was at Laurence Corner, and she never considered departing from it.

Natalie Kiley, the beauty of transformation (Theme Traders' project manager):

"It's an astonishing thing, being able to turn an empty space into something wonderful in just a few days. If you're an interior designer working on a house, it might take six months or a year to see the result, but with a party, you have a few days to see something created from nothing, to transform an ordinary garden into something out of Arabian nights. It's so cool."

In much the same way as dogs are said to resemble their owners, so Laurence Corner was made in the image of Victor Jamilly – non-conformist, eclectic, and in a league of its own. Victor, like his father before him (and, as it would turn out, his children after him) was a maverick. He wanted to do his own thing in his own way, when it suited him. While others ,who'd jumped on the army surplus bandwagon, started forming syndicates to control the trade and bulk-buy en masse, Victor was content to be outside of the circle, running Laurence Corner as his own personal Aladdin's Cave, choosing stock more according to personal whim than market forces.

Either by luck or design, Laurence Corner continued to thrive throughout the decades after its somewhat unspectacular inception. The clientele was eclectic, the location – just down the road from trendy Capital Radio – buzzing, and the ever-changing, unpredictable nature of the stock made it more like working in a theatre than a retail establishment. Both David and Kim learned invaluable lessons about sales, display and style, as well as supply and demand. However, they were not in the remotest hurry to put these to any practical use in terms of starting up businesses of their own. Laurence Corner was in many ways a mink-lined coffin; it provided just enough stimulation and opportunity for creativity that the duo didn't feel either stifled or thwarted. Why would they look for work elsewhere when they were already positioned at the very centre of what was going on?

Besides, each had their own life outside work which occupied much of their energy. David started to dabble in deals that his father shied away from, like buying 3000 Swedish army coats with his friend Michael White, which proved an outstanding success when he sold them on, in bulk, making a hefty profit.

He had also set up his own charity, called POD, providing parties for children in hospital. The idea had come about, as such things do, in a roundabout way. Possessed of a highly developed social conscience, he'd begun by doing voluntary work with the Samaritans, then the elderly, then with abused women and their children. This had segued into arranging children's parties in hospitals – then an untried concept. He coordinated everything including the entertainer, and went along to make sure everything ran smoothly. With his own life so relatively straightforward and untroubled, it was his way of giving something back.

Kim and Michel had successfully bought and sold a series of properties, finally acquiring their dream house – an open-plan former artist's studio in Hampstead Garden Suburb, surrounded by trees and approached by way of an overgrown church path.

How Kim and Michel got their dream house (despite all the obstacles). A lesson in buying and selling

When Kim cycled off to look at the studio house and fell in love with it on the spot, Mrs Rosenthal, the owner, told her there was already an offer on it, from the estate agent's girlfriend no less. Dejectedly she cycled home and called Michel, who was away at the time, to tell him the bad news. Michel, a disciple of the 'it ain't over 'til it's over' school of thought, refused to give up. "Go back and tell Mrs Rosenthal that you want to buy it. Ask her to give you a date when the other people should have exchanged contract, and get her to agree that if they don't, she'll sell it to you." Dutifully, Kim got back on her bike. The agreed date arrived. Kim once again called Mrs Rosenthal who told her: "They haven't exchanged yet, but they're very close." "But you said you'd sell it to us." Ah yes, that was true… Kim and Michel exchanged contracts on the house that same day, without structural surveys, mortgages or much in the way of pre-sale nerves, and Kim learned 3 important life/business lessons:

- never take 'no' for an answer
- be persistent, even when the odds are against you
- if opportunity presents itself, seize it fast.

The POD squad

POD was inspired by David's own boyhood memories of visits to hospital to be treated for asthma. To a small child, hospitals were big, scary places where time dragged at the pace of an arthritic snail – too little to do and too much time to think. Fast forward twenty odd years and what could be more appropriate for a young man with a flair for the theatrical, a big circle of friends which boasted more than a smattering of actors, musicians and magicians and a well developed social conscience than to set up a charity running free children's parties in hospital wards?

POD began in 1977 with a party at Great Ormond Street Hospital. "We've no idea what you're actually on about," was the response to David's attempts to explain his new concept, "but why don't you come in and give it a go?"

David still remembers the buzz of that first event. "We did a show that was really basic – simple magic tricks, balloon making, singing – and immediately you saw the kids relaxing and being distracted from whatever was wrong with them. The nurses, who didn't have a clue who these strange people clogging up their ward were, could see an immediate, positive reaction."

The POD party was an instant hit and became a monthly event. Word soon spread to other hospitals in London and further afield and now, decades later, POD entertainers – still funded entirely by the charity under the expert guidance of Margaret Munford, POD's tireless Administrator for the last twenty years – provide over 2000 shows a year. Such shows have uplifted over 500,000 children, to date, including the 10-year-old patient, who wrote this letter:

"I wasn't feeling very well but when Mr Merlin came to visit me, he really cheered me up. He was lovely, funny and kind. Mr Merlin gave me two balls and then I had six coming out of my hand. I was very shocked that so many balls came out of my hand and my mammy and the nurses were very puzzled."

In the larger world, however, self-interest was the order of the day. Thatcher's Britain spawned a generation who believed in lip-gloss, shoulder pads and free enterprise. Shaggy perms were in, feather cuts were out. Society was changing, but inside the shop on the corner of Hampstead Road, things stayed more or less the same. People still came searching for the quirky and unique, boxes still piled up in the basement, strange people still lurked by the straightjacket display. But, towards the end of the 1980s, something happened which jolted the Jamillys' world squarely off its axis.

Following the death of Kim and David's much-loved mum Audrey, Victor had remarried (to another Kim, just to be confusing) and decided his new wife was exactly the breath of fresh air Laurence Corner needed. The result was that Victor began introducing changes and David, who had devoted nearly two decades to the army surplus emporium, had his nose put most determinedly out of joint. He realised he had three choices:

- Stay on, bite his lip and accept that things had changed
- Stay on, work out his options and leave as soon as he had something better to go to.
- Dramatically announce he was quitting, in the hope that his shocked dad would realise how indispensable he was and beg him to stay.

Not yet being the astute businessman he would later become, David overlooked option 2 (the correct answer) and plumped instead for option 3. On handing in his notice, he was somewhat nonplussed to realise that, not only was his father not about to fall to his knees and beg him not to go, he actually seemed to be encouraging him to leave, agreeing that maybe it was time his son spread his wings a little. Still, David reasoned as he walked out of the Laurence Corner door for what he fully expected would not to be the last time, his father would soon change his tune when he saw how lost the place was without him. All he had to do was sit back and wait.

Meanwhile, Kim was facing a crossroads of her own. She too had found the new order difficult to get used to, particularly since Kim (the second) was around her own age. With David gone, and with clear signs that her stepmother would eventually start working at the store, she felt increasingly sidelined and adrift from the sheltering cocoon that Laurence Corner formerly represented. There are few things lonelier than feeling an outsider in a place that one has always thought of as home, and Kim soon found herself looking enviously at her older brother's newly-acquired (though not entirely welcomed) liberty and wondering just how hard it could be to strike off on her own. Conveniently ignoring the fact that she had just turned thirty, with no discernible qualifications and only one long-term job to her name, Kim decided to follow David's example and resign from Laurence Corner. She had no plans, savings or big ideas, but she was confident something would turn up. All she had to do was wait.

The Jamilly siblings, it has to be said, put a lot of faith in waiting.

Insider tip: Leaving do's (and don'ts):

Off to seek professional pastures new? Whatever the circumstances, you'll be wanting a send off that no one is likely to forget....

- DON'T organise your own – chances are you'll be self-effacingly half-hearted about it and besides, you want to be able to relax and enjoy it. Instead, hand over responsibility to someone you trust.
- DO try to pick a venue that's separate from the workplace, so that people have a chance to unwind, but one that offers enough privacy for speeches. A private room in a pub or a restaurant is perfect, or failing that, a sectioned off area.
- DON'T arrange an event on a Friday night as there's more chance of people having to rush off, even if that is the official leaving day.
- DO structure the evening carefully so that the speeches and presentation come when people have had enough time to loosen up after work, but not so much time that half of them are either gone or comatose!
- DO make the evening as personal as possible. Decorate the venue with enlarged photos of the

guest of honour and other staff members, organise a scrap book of memories and mementos which can be circulated during the evening.

- DON'T forget, this is a work-related occasion, so while former colleagues should be on the guest list, too many personal friends from a non-professional sphere will change the atmosphere and might affect the feeling of camaraderie.

- DO pre-book a taxi for the guest of honour and provide a couple of large carrier bags to transport cards, flowers etc.

CHAPTER THREE
spaceman sam and the red elephant

Waiting proved not to be nearly as easy a strategy as David and Kim had envisioned.

For David, nursing serious wounds to both his pride and his bank balance, there was the question of cash flow. Or lack thereof. For Kim, who was married to diamond dealer Michel so had fewer financial pressures, the problems were more about how to fill the hours. Enforced leisure time had never been her strong point.

An experienced biker, David decided he was going to find work as a motorbike courier. He had a notion that he'd enjoy the freedom of the open road, the informality of an irregular timetable (not to mention the chance of spending quality time with his beloved Harley Davidson). On his first day, he was given a list of thirty jobs. What he didn't know was that this was a test – no one did that many jobs in a day. Especially in the rain. Without any experience. When he staggered back at the end of the day, with a record thirty signatures on his list, his legs seriously wobbly, the operators and other couriers gazed at him open-mouthed before breaking into a round of applause. He had won his spurs.

But the life of a motorcycle courier wasn't all it had appeared to be. Though David quickly rose to be head-honcho driver, spending the day riding around London's congested and often rain-sodden streets, wasn't quite what he'd imagined for himself.

Sitting at home in the splendour of the house she shared with Michel in Hampstead Garden Suburb, Kim too was finding the waiting game harder than she'd thought. Clearly, being a lady of leisure was an acquired skill – and she had yet to acquire it. She endeavoured to keep busy in two ways:

- writing to all the contacts in her filofax to inform them that she was open to offers and
- watching the spiders on her ceiling building their webs.

It was when she realised she was spending far more time on the second activity than the first and had even, worryingly, begun naming her arachnid friends, that she decided something had to be done.

How Kim realised she'd become obsessed:

"My favourite pastime was to lie on my bed and stare at the ceiling, which was, by the way, very enchanting, and draped with multiple gargantuan spider webs. Delicately woven and slightly grey on most of the corners, they attached themselves to the windows and light-fittings, dangling like angel hair from the rafters as they swayed in the breeze. Fred, our master spider was huge and we enjoyed a daily ritual whereby I chased him out of the bath with a sheet of A4 paper, only to find him right back waiting for me the next morning. He became like a friend." Uh-oh.

Meanwhile, David, in addition to speeding around town in black leathers, had been devoting time to POD. It was while he was on the children's wards, accompanying the entertainers he'd hired that he started picking up ideas and wondering just how difficult this could be. Tentatively, he started entertaining at the parties himself – doing a bit of magic, playing the guitar. What he discovered was that if you engage children in theatre – whether it's through costumes, effects or atmosphere – you've won them over.

He developed a character, Spaceman Sam, clad (predictably) in a spacesuit with helmet. The costume provided a convenient barrier, which shielded his more unassuming, everyday self from public scrutiny and gave a platform to a louder, brasher alter ego. The kids responded and little by little an idea was born. Why not become a children's party entertainer? Set your own hours, be your own boss. And what was the one thing better than a children's party entertainer? Two children's party entertainers of course! Someone else to share the responsibility, the profits, the noise. Which is how Kim came to be roped in.

With David already in character as Spaceman Sam, Kim had to come up with her own identity. It would be interesting to catalogue here, the in-depth, conceptual processes that went into creating the character of Red Elephant, which Kim eventually evolved. Interesting, but not entirely accurate. Basically the red elephant came about by economic rather than creative design. The elephant costume – metres of red fabric with a long trunk stuffed with wadding and a matching skinny tail – was being sold off cheap in the classifieds of The Stage magazine. So what if it was hot and sweaty and was the sartorial equivalent of spending half a day in the steam room? It was an identifiable children's character. Now all she and

David had to do was place an advert in the local paper and wait... (again).

* * *

That first week, the requests came flooding in – well, two anyway, and a new career path began in the lives of the Jamilly siblings. They quickly developed a formula for keeping the children occupied – half an hour's magic, followed by face painting, then food and games, then a little magic to end with, all for the knock-down price of £250 (including food).

Keeping twenty odd children amused for three hours is no mean feat, but David developed a cunning strategy for dealing with any bolshy or over-e-numbered party guests – invite them to bash the Red Elephant. This doubled as a way for seriously hyper kids to unleash some pent up energy *and* for David to get his own back on Kim who irritatingly refused to get as tense as him about the whole business of party entertaining.

Gary Davison (childhood friend):

"My household where I lived with my mum was pretty conservative, and David's seemed very exotic by comparison. David's bedroom featured a little cubbyhole plastered with psychedelic posters where half a dozen people could squeeze in at a time. We were always piling in there, listening to music full blast and generally thinking we were pretty cool."

David's favourite ruse was to pick up his guitar and invite the party guests to fall into line behind the Red Elephant for a conga. Whenever the music stopped, he'd tell them to lay into the Red Elephant. It was very hot in the Red Elephant suit. Let alone being bashed by a multitude of excitable children, while doing the Conga. At the end of the song, depending on exactly how irritated he was feeling, David was quite likely to say, "As that was *so* much fun, let's do it all again". Sometimes it was just as well the costume covered Kim's expression.

The parties were a big hit and the bookings stacked up. They started to get requests for themed parties and invested in a 6ft palm tree as a prop for the ever-popular tropical/beach/pirate theme. Instantly, it became clear that themed events were a very good idea, instantaneously creating the holy party trilogy of 'Expectation, Drama and Bonding'.

Why theme an event?

- **Expectation:** "If we have the budget we'll be thinking of teasers months and months ahead," says David. "The invitation won't be a piece of paper, it'll be a shoe with a script inside. The reminder won't be a piece of card, it'll be some intriguing object left on your doorstep. That builds the expectation. You're excited, you want to find out where this is leading."

- **Drama:** "You have to have that 'wow' thing when you come through the door," says Kim. "I had a horror party at my house and there was a vampire hanging upside down from a tree as guests came in the gate.

Or we had a Space party with a funny Yoda character,
or an Africa party with a gorilla. That touch of
theatre immediately tells guests that they're entering
a different world, that the event is going to be an
escape from reality."

- **Bonding:** A theme provides an instant ice-breaker,
as well as a great bonding-mechanism. How could you
not smile at other guests when you're all dressed up
in hula skirts or seventies garb? Immediately there's
a sense of being a part of something, a member of a
select group all bound by a common experience.

Theming children's parties involves another two crucial
elements – simplicity and mystery. Let's face it, a party is about
having fun and it's not much fun if you have to stand there while
a concept is explained to you, when all you want to do is jump
up and down wearing an eye patch and poke your friends with a
plastic sword. The mystery element comes in with hide and seek
or cleverly-laid treasure hunts – kids love nothing better than
finding something that's hidden, and a well-laid trail of clues can
take up a big chunk of entertainment time.

If Kim and David had had a business plan at this point, which
of course they didn't, it would have consisted of just three words,
Kim's favourite motto: 'never say no'. If opportunities came their
way – whether it was parties, or buying and selling a job lot of
second hand wedding dresses – they took them.

One of the more bizarre jobs offered to them was doing the
Christmas grotto at Whiteleys shopping centre in London.
David was obviously Father Christmas, while Kim would be one
of Santa's elves. How hard could it be?

Well, the first thing that didn't go quite to plan was Santa's big arrival. The idea was to have a security guard dressed as Father Christmas abseil down the central atrium in the mall and disappear into the grotto where he'd seamlessly be replaced by David, who'd reappear and start the show. All started well, with the fake Santa shinning over the top balcony and lowering himself on a rope to the next floor down, and the next… except that each time he went down a floor, his beard got caught in the winching mechanism. The only way to free him was for Kim to scuttle from one level to the next wielding a pair of scissors with which to snip away more and more of the snowy-white beard. By the time he arrived at the bottom, he was the cleanest shaven of Santas, a Hugh Grant among Father Christmases. Not surprisingly, when David quickly substituted for him, the assembled children smelled a rat.

"How come you've grown your beard back so quick?" replaced 'Can I have the red Transformer?' as the question of the day from visitors to the grotto.

David also entertained at Harvester pubs on Sunday lunchtimes for £50 a time (the second platform of the non-existent business plan being 'no job too small'), travelling from North London to Gillingham in Kent to perform magic tricks, while customers munched through gammon steaks or flame-grilled chicken.

Bernard O'Neill, the restaurant manager who hired him (and who went on to become a life-long friend), remembers David being a big hit with two particular groups. "He went down very well with women and children. One woman fell madly in love with him and used to book a table whenever he was there, gazing up at him lovingly over her Sunday roast. And he was a crowd puller with the kids as well. I was immediately struck by his unlimited patience."

At one point, the ever-resourceful David even did a stint as a sing-o-gram, wearing a rather silly hat and singing a poem Kim had written on the back of a beer-mat.

In the meantime, Kim, during 'resting periods' as the Red Elephant, was still patiently working through her old contacts, announcing her continuing availability for gainful employment. Eventually, her persistence paid off when she received a call from Richard, her erstwhile Laurence Corner client, who'd been so impressed with her room-decorating a few years back. He knew she'd become involved in organising parties and wondered if she wanted to come along to pitch at a meeting for a big corporate event. Listening to him explain that this was the very prestigious awards ceremony for TV-am, to be held at London's Alexandra Palace, Kim couldn't help but wonder if he quite grasped that the limit of her party organising skills thus far had been doing the conga dressed as an elephant, but she wisely refrained from mentioning it.

On the appointed day, she turned up for the meeting at the imposing Alexandra Palace and was shown into a large boardroom, around which sat twelve serious looking people in

Kim's top 3 tips on how NOT to be intimidated in meetings:

- Dress the part (where possible reflect the dress-code of the people you're meeting with).
- Make eye contact (in an open rather than a crazed way).
- Say something early on.

suits. Richard, who was chairing the meeting, explained that the event would cater for 800 guests (at this Kim gulped loudly and slid slightly further down in her seat) and would need everything from flower arrangers to stage managers. The theme of the night was to be a fairground, so they'd also need to find fairground stalls and performers to man them.

When it came to asking who was interested in being involved, Richard started small.

"Who'd like to organise the stage plants?" Thinking she must be seen to be proactive, Kim put her hand up.

Finding it surprisingly painless, she decided to keep putting her hand up. By the end of the meeting, she was slightly taken aback to discover she'd volunteered to organise six full size fairground stalls, all the stall holders, six performers, including fortune tellers, plus of course the plants. Incredibly, she managed not to choke when she was told her part of the budget – a cool £12,000.

Ever the optimist, she convinced herself that this was nothing she couldn't handle. Just because she had next to no experience of large-scale events, there was no reason to panic. It'd be just like the children's parties – except scaled up by a factor of a hundred. First thing she needed was some fairground stalls and someone to come and set them up. She made a few phone calls and was put in touch with someone called Dickie, which probably ought to have set alarm bells ringing. Dickie promised her the moon and, having left him a deposit, Kim walked away smugly convinced that there was nothing to this events management lark as long as one was prepared to think big and seize the day.

But when Dickie failed to call back to confirm times, or to show up in any of the places he was supposed to, Kim began to feel ever so slightly nervous. "They don't call him Tricky

Dickie for nothing," she was told cheerfully at one of the designated meeting spots where her contact once again failed to materialise.

Kim thought about the promises she'd made, all the commitments she'd given. She thought about the money, and all the people she'd be letting down. Then she did what any grown up, sensible businesswoman would do. She rang her big brother.

David was her rock, she reasoned. He was always calm, always knew what to do. He'd reassure her that it was all perfectly achievable. She showed him the quote she'd given to the event organisers. He turned slightly pale.

"What the f*** have you done?"

It wasn't quite the response she was looking for.

Still, David liked nothing more than a challenge. He decided that, since it was proving so difficult to procure a ready-made fairground, the easiest thing was to make one themselves, from scratch. Within a day he had rounded up a motley line-up of assorted creative friends and they'd begun.

Of course, like all seemingly straightforward projects, there were hidden catches. Like the fact that, since Alexandra Palace had famously burned to the ground in 1873 and been rebuilt only to suffer another devastating fire in 1980, everything they used to make the stalls had to be fire retardant, including the paint and materials.

The centre of operations was Kim's house (in Hampstead Garden Suburb) where the open plan layout and tree-screened garden lent themselves to creativity on a grand scale. Kim was responsible for stitching together industrial quantities of red and white striped material to make the overhead canopies and sides for the stalls. David's artist friend, Rob Olins, now a well known sculptor and artist, was in charge of painting, helped by willing, if largely unskilled, volunteers like Michel. Not only the wooden structures, but also Kim's parquet floor and kitchen surfaces received a bright new coat of acrylic paint.

Incredibly, within days, the structures were beginning to take shape, vividly coloured wooden stalls with beautiful hand-painted designs and sweeping, draped canopies. But there were still the other things on the list that Kim had so confidently volunteered for – like supplying all the party foliage.

The only person Kim knew who had a clue about plants was Andrew, who managed the Camden Garden Centre from where she'd mostly restocked her garden. She decided to pay him a visit. The garden centre was a riot of colour when she walked in, with row upon row of roses in full bloom.

"Andrew, what happens to these roses at night?" Kim ventured, innocently.

If he found it a strange question, Andrew kept his bafflement hidden.

"Nothing," he replied slowly.

"So they wouldn't really be missed if they disappeared from here for, say, half a day and a night?"

Before he quite knew what had hit him, Andrew found himself agreeing not only to 'lend' Kim hundreds of prime condition rose bushes in their pots, but also to bring them to Alexandra Palace himself and supervise their installation.

As Michel – part time diamond dealer, full time concerned husband – gazed on in open bemusement, Kim once again demonstrated the truth of that simple golden business/life rule: If you don't ask, you won't get.

Next on the list were the performers. Not only had Kim promised to provide the fairground equipment, she'd also committed to finding people to man the stalls, and to mill around in costume mingling with the party guests and providing a dash of authentic colour. So they had to be outgoing and have a certain amount of dramatic flair. Where better to look than amongst the ranks of 'resting' actors. Kim and David duly took out an advert in the back of thespian bible, *The Stage,* advertising for performers for a forthcoming event. Auditions were held in the duo's London office, aka upstairs at the Punch and Judy pub in Covent Garden.

The first two would-be fairground personnel were fresh out of drama school and working part time as singing flower girls in Covent Garden. Orla was presented with a set of tarot cards and asked to feign a reading. "Oh I already know how to read the cards," she said airily. The fact that she somehow failed to spot that the death card had been strategically removed from the pack (on the grounds that being presented with their own mortality might get in the way of the guests having a good time) kind of put paid to her claims of superior knowledge, but she got the part. Her friend Maz, who was charged with reading palms, was from the Good News Only school of fortune telling and happily foretold health, happiness and untold wealth to the assembled panel before blowing things slightly by assuring Michel – there only to support his wife – that he would shortly be meeting the love of his life.

By the end of that night, Kim and David had their dream team of dedicated performers to add to their impressive collection of borrowed rose bushes and painstakingly hand-crafted fairground stalls. Now all that remained was to sit back and enjoy the event itself.

Except that of course they couldn't do anything of the sort. Orchestrating their part of the awards ceremony party at Alexandra Palace involved all of their powers of ingenuity, creativity, spontaneity and stamina. There were the stalls to set up, the roses to position, the performers to prepare. Then there was the actual party itself, where everyone had different roles to play, with David and Kim taking their turn behind the stalls, as well as keeping a sharp eye on their 'staff'. A hairy moment where palm-reading novice Maz read for celebrity fortune teller Russell Grant turned quickly into triumph when the TV star congratulated her on her intuition and insight. And afterwards, at 2am when the last of the delighted party-goers had left, and Kim had been congratulated for the hundredth time on pulling the metaphorical rabbit out of the hat, there were still the stalls to be dismantled and the roses safely loaded into Andrew's van.

Party piece: Keith the Thief

One of the characters Kim and David hired for the TV-am party was a pick pocket called Keith the Thief. During the course of the party, he picked the pockets of many of the celebrity guests, including the late, great Jeremy Beadle, whose wallet happened to contain his latest television contract stating exactly how much he was getting paid. "Surely that's not all, Jeremy?" Keith shrieked, in mock outrage to the somewhat embarrassed amusement of the TV prankster.

By the time they finally got home, Kim and David were exhausted – but elated. By the skin of their teeth, they'd managed to create a different world where party guests had left reality at the door and entered for a few hours into a fantasy of make-believe. The atmosphere had been electric and, from the comments they'd had all night, the event had been a resounding success.

Things to remember when throwing a fancy dress party (part two)

- Start by throwing together a box of extra dressing up props handy for anyone who has forgotten, or just not bothered.
- When setting a theme, bear in mind you'll probably want to decorate the venue in line with the costumes, so a beach party (sand, surf boards, parasols) or a black and white party, is going to be easier than, say a 1950s party or an outer space party.
- On the whole, guests want to feel glamorous, whatever the theme – it's still a party after all – so try to steer clear of themes like 'bad taste'.
- As the host/hostess you'll be expected to set the tone for the whole event so make sure your own outfit is stunning. You're likely to be greeting your guests at the door, so you'll be the first thing they see – push the boat out!
- If guests have made a real effort to dress up, they're going to want some kind of photographic record of the night, so make sure you take plenty of pictures. Arranging a group shot of all the guests in their finery is a great way of bringing people together.

By luck, adventurousness and sheer chutzpah, they'd stumbled across something they were actually very good at, something which combined their love of theatre, their experience of props and costumes and their entrepreneurial heritage. Though it was 1990 and event management had yet to be recognised as a job description, let alone as the multi-million pound industry it would become, they had blundered into a field which they instinctively understood. As they dropped off to sleep that night, exhausted but euphoric, they had no idea that they'd just embarked on the next great venture of their lives.

CHAPTER FOUR
getting the party started

The TV-am party brought about two important changes in David and Kim's lives:

- they were now the proud owners of a set of hand-decorated, fully functioning fair-ground stalls and
- they now had an understanding of how big budget event planning worked.

The £12,000 figure which had at first seemed so preposterous, had been broken down into individual components so that the client could see exactly where the money was going. Once the Jamillys had got over the number of noughts involved, they were able to recognise that essentially the formula was the same as with the children's parties they'd been putting on for the past two years, only on a slightly bigger scale:

- Create a buzz of anticipation and excitement about the event.
- Grab guests' attention the second they come through the door.
- Make sure they have a 'wow' experience that they've never had elsewhere.

Armed with the formula and the fairground stalls, David and Kim started spreading the word and taking bookings for other parties with a fairground theme. It was the very beginning of the 1990s and no one had really heard of themed parties before – at least not in the sense of having props, costumes, performers, even food themed to the event. The Jamillys, in keeping with family tradition, had found themselves more by luck than judgement, in at the beginning of a market trend. And now it was up to them to capitalise on it.

For the next couple of years they, and their little band of freelance performers, took their fairground party round the country. Little by little, the UK woke up to the idea that an event didn't have to be either a stiff stand-up drinks party or a chaotic thrown-together gathering but instead could be a holistic knitting together of all the elements that make up a social event into one cohesive, theatrical experience. In other words, a party could be a production. David and Kim could hardly believe their luck. They'd stumbled upon a market still in its embryonic stages, but nevertheless on the cusp of taking off, and moreover, a market that encompassed both their experience of children's parties AND their love of theatre, costume and design. Bingo!

This was the moment when the Jamillys started to realise that parties could be more than a stop-gap money-earner while they waited for their 'real' business lives to begin; they could actually, rather incredibly, be an end in themselves.

Slowly but surely, they started to see themselves less as two individuals randomly reacting to opportunities that cropped up in their path, and more of a skilled unit with a commodity to offer. And what does every skilled unit with a commodity to offer need? A bloody good name.

In their makeshift office on the mezzanine level of Kim's open-plan studio house, the duo agonised over a suitable moniker for their fledgling enterprise. And when their agonising got too heated, which it frequently did, Michel – a late riser, who would often be languishing in bed in full view (and earshot) of the mezzanine office – would join in.

Kim came up with the word Traders, which seemed to sum up their entrepreneurial heritage and their sense of having something of value to offer, but they knew there was another word lacking. 'Fair' would have been an appropriate option, as the fairground was proving such a great source of income. And it's true to say that calling themselves 'fair traders' back in the early 1990s, would have put them way ahead of the times. But something made them realise that defining their company by the fairground stalls would be too restrictive because, while too much of a good thing can often be an even better thing, it can also start to wear thin. So they decided on the broader word 'theme', which provided more flexibility AND handily began with the letter T, thus producing the pleasing alliterative abbreviation TT.

Now they were a bona fide company, they had to get an accountant.

"What kind of business are you in?" asked the one they were eventually recommended.

"Parties," they replied.

The accountant's pen hovered uncertainly over the form he was filling in. This being 1990, there was no box to tick for 'parties'. Could they be pulling his leg, he wondered nervously?

Outside the narrow constraints of the financial world, however, the concept of managed events was starting to gain ground.

The fairground stalls introduced partygoers to the idea that an event could be a theatrical experience, but once they'd had a chance to assimilate that new concept, their expectations began to become more sophisticated.

"What else have you got?" clients began asking.

The short answer to that was 'not a lot', but in keeping with their 'never say no' principle, David and Kim began developing other party themes. They put together a brochure for their fledgling company, based on ideas that only existed inside their own imaginations. They'd present them to the client as a fait accompli. Then if anyone expressed an interest, they'd have to figure out how on earth to do them. They added a Wild West theme to their repertoire, and a Hollywood theme.

"We have a Marilyn lookalike walking down a boulevard," Kim would tell prospective clients. Then she'd have to go back to David and confess:

"The good news is, I've got a booking for another party. The bad news is we need a Marilyn lookalike AND a boulevard. By Saturday."

Often the clients themselves would drive the creativity, constantly coming back with the pressing question "what else have you got?". Rather than have to admit "er, not a lot" they'd come up with something that fed into whatever the client had last expressed an interest in. "You thought the Round the World Cruise party was good – what about a Walking on the Ceiling party?" (cue Kim: "A walking on the WHAT party?")

While Theme Traders was still just David and Kim (and occasionally Michel's disembodied voice wafting up to the mezzanine level), they collected a wide pool of freelance performers and technicians they could call on to help as and when events arose. But it was never a case of turning up at a venue in time for an event then buggering off again; everyone they employed helped load vans, drive them, set up lights and

The growth-cycle of a party theme

- Think of an idea that offers both opportunities for glamour (let's face it no one really wants to go to a party dressed like an Ork from Lord of the Rings) and for variety, for example a Round the World Cruise theme.
- Come up with a wow element or a 'talking point', inspired by the chosen theme, for when guests first arrive; in this case, getting them to enter through turnstiles and be searched by customs officers
- Work out a structure for the theme – like dividing the room into five sections, each representing a different continent.
- Decide how to bring that structure to life. Australia? How about having someone playing the didgeridoo? Perfect. Europe? Recreate the Eiffel Tower.
- Only once the client has signed on the dotted line are you allowed to start panicking about how to put into practice what your imagination has created. Like the small matter of finding a didgeridoo... or someone to play it...

scenery, cart props around, as well as de-rigging at the end of the night. Often friends, finding themselves with some spare time on their hands, would offer to help out with a particular event or theme, both as a favour to Kim and David (*primary motive)* and also so they could go back to the more mundane day job and say airily "on my day off I handed out drinks at a party dressed as a giant bumble bee" (*secret motive*).

Bernard O'Neill (businessman):

"David asked me to help at an early party where we were to make Margaritas. I'd never made one in my life and guessed at the quantities we'd require with the result that I completely over-ordered on the tequila and we made four bin-loads of lethal-strength cocktails. Mind you, no one complained at the time – in fact they kept coming back for more. I think there were a few sore heads the next day though."

Every fresh theme entailed making new props and costumes. There were backdrops to be painted and rigging erected. And all these things needed to be stored. The Jamillys rented a garage on Rosemary Avenue in nearby Finchley to house all their equipment, and when the door of that would no longer shut, they rented another one… and another one… and another…

David and Kim, who still thought of the parties as a good wheeze to make some money until their real business opportunity came along, found themselves working longer and longer hours. Their daily work-schedule looked something like this:

9am: convene on the mezzanine at Kim's studio, which also doubled as the Theme Traders office, facing each other across a desk, while Michel lay in bed down below reading the FT.

9.30am–3pm: argue loudly about themes, props, budgets,

attempting to force Michel to take sides (although naturally he was far too sensible to do anything of the sort).

3pm: visit the garages, checking on the condition of the stock and sorting out the props and equipment needed for that night's event.

4pm: load up the van

5pm: arrive at the venue and set up

12am: finish and pack away

3am: unpack the equipment into the garages

4am: drop exhausted into bed, ready to do the whole thing all over again in just five hours time.

It was a punishing regime, and Kim and David had to get used to being on call 24-hours a day, but the bookings continued to flood in, and the duo found that, much to their surprise, they were starting to make some serious money. Like their dad with his sailors' bellbottoms and their granddad with his cinema projector, they'd found a product people actually wanted and had been lucky enough to be in the right place at the right time. Society was changing. New working legislation meant many people had more leisure time than before. And more to the point, the eighties, with their glitz and glamour, shoulder pads and wine bars, had shattered that widely-held notion that showing off, particularly where money was concerned, was somehow un-British. Suddenly, it seemed like everyone was getting richer – and they wanted everyone else to know about it.

Parties were back in fashion – the bigger and bolder the better.

Of course, at that stage, David and Kim had no idea of the wider sociological implications of the newfound national obsession with staging extravagant events. All they knew was that the phone didn't stop ringing – and that if they did three parties a week, that was over two thousand quid. Plus the more events they did, the bigger their collection of costumes and props, which could also be hired out separately to other event organisers or directly to the companies staging the events.

The Jamillys' collection of rented garages grew along with their client base, and by the time they were into double figures, it occurred to them that they might actually have to start thinking about buying some premises, rather than just renting more and more lock ups. Tentatively, they set themselves a target of making £25,000 clear profit over a period of 12 months, to put towards a deposit on a building – a ridiculous sum for a pair who, just a couple of years before, had been playing Harvester gigs at £50 a time. When it became clear that figure was achievable, they doubled it to £50,000. To their amazement, target-setting seemed to really work.

How to set effective targets

- Start small – achieving targets gives you the confidence to set bigger ones the next time.
- Set a definite time limit (leaving them open ended removes the momentum to succeed)
- WRITE THEM DOWN. "If you write something down and then don't achieve it, you end up feeling very stupid," says David. "It's easier just to meet the target."

It was in 1994, four years after the TV-am party, that Theme Traders counted up and realised they were paying rent on 60 lock up garages in and around North London, to house their ever mushrooming collection of stock. The time had come, they realised, rather queasily adding together the rows and rows of figures, to bite the bullet and buy their own place.

By now they had the £50,000 they'd already set as a target to put down as a deposit and they were confident they could secure a mortgage to buy premises big enough to accommodate their unwieldy business. Even though he had little real idea of what exactly they did, their local bank manager decided to indulge them. After all, a business based on parties and having fun sounded quite glamorous. They duly trawled around the less attractive areas of North West London looking for a building large enough to act as storehouse, showroom, workshop and company offices. Finally they found the perfect place – an abandoned duffel coat factory with various outbuildings in the unglamorous environs of Oaklands Road, Cricklewood. It had previously served as a roller skating rink, a World War I recreational club, an Irish dancehall and a hardware wholesaler and was now going for the princely sum of £150,000.

The day arrived for the exchange of contracts and it was a momentous occasion all round. Not only were David and Kim committing to the biggest purchase of their lives, but they were also booked to do a party for the opening of the Virgin Atlantic Hong Kong route, at which Richard Branson was to be guest of honour, a very prestigious coup for the still fledgling company. It would be no exaggeration to say nerves were ever so slightly frayed.

It was decided that David would go onsite to oversee the party, while Kim would remain behind supervising the property exchange. Both procedures had been meticulously planned. Everything was completely straightforward... except, of course, for the things that weren't.

The first sign of a problem came when Kim rang David, her voice cracking with rage.

"The regional manager of the bank has intervened and he won't lend us the money." She was so furious she could hardly talk.

The local bank manager, who had promised to lend them the £100,000 extra they needed to buy the Cricklewood building, had been overruled at the last minute by his boss who, unable to grasp the strange, new concept of event management, had deemed the Jamillys too much of a risk.

Kim, who'd rebelled against authority since schooldays, and who viewed the word 'no' as a personal challenge to be tackled full on, was predictably incensed.

"Let's tell them to stuff their money, we'll do it on our own," she fumed.

David, inclined to be less impetuous than his sister, was on this occasion in complete agreement. They would go ahead with the exchange, putting down their £50,000 deposit as agreed, and pray that they could raise the remaining £100,000 before the completion day four weeks hence.

"No."

"Pardon?"

It had been bad enough when the bank refused them a loan for the extra money, but now it seemed they were also refusing to release Kim and David's own funds. At first, Kim thought she must have misheard.

"It would be professionally irresponsible of us to release the money for exchange without having the rest of the capital in place to complete."

Kim was dumbfounded.

"But it's our money, and we're telling you to release it."

The bank wouldn't budge.

David, standing in a phone box outside the venue for the Virgin Atlantic party, was outraged.

"Tell them we'll sue!"

As the clock ticked, Kim appealed to the bank manager, at first cajoling, then arguing and finally demanding, but to little effect. They were given a 24-hour extension to exchange contracts. That night, as the Virgin Atlantic party went ahead, to great acclaim, Kim and David agonised about the ludicrousness of the situation. They were on the brink of losing out on the property they wanted because they were being denied access to their own money. How could that be right?

It wasn't until the afternoon of the following day, following endless heated arguments, that David, and a by now nearly apoplectic Kim, finally managed to convince their highly disapproving bank manager to release their funds. Needless to say, he immediately became their ex bank-manager. Now there was just the small matter of raising £100,000 in four weeks...

For many people, that kind of pressure would have been intolerable, but the Jamilly siblings had always operated according to a different code of principles: arriving at a commitment was the hard part, meeting it was a walk in the park. Mum and Dad, Audrey and Victor had brought them up to understand that once they agreed to something, there simply was no option for not carrying it through. One way or another the deal would be completed.

Kim set about ringing every bank she could find. The problem they came up against was that event management in 1994 wasn't the influential, well known industry it would later become. In fact, few people outside of the hospitality world had even heard of it. Most bank managers still thought of parties as a few people dressed in their best clothes, dancing in the kitchen to a cassette player, or standing around in a flock-wallpapered room above a pub, drinking warm white wine and passing round peanuts. So asking bank managers for a mortgage of £100,000 based on a party business required a huge leap of faith.

But if there's one thing guaranteed to galvanise Kim into action, it's the desire to prove the doubters wrong. She continued making appointments and explaining to bemused men in suits exactly what it was she and David did, why people wanted party planners and just how much people were prepared to pay for their services.

It worked. By the time the four-week deadline was up, Kim had persuaded an unusually forward-thinking bank to take a gamble that the event management business was going to prove more than a flash in the pan. Soon after, Theme Traders became the proud owner of 600m^2 of draughty warehouse space in unfashionable Cricklewood.

They were on their way.

CHAPTER FIVE

becoming grown ups

Once the euphoria of having a great big set of jangly keys to their own premises, not to mention all their stock under one roof, had subsided, David and Kim became aware of a rather uncomfortable thought. Now that they had their own premises, shouldn't they be hiring some staff to man those premises?

It was not something either had much experience in. Up until then, they'd been the sole staff members of Theme Traders, relying on a pool of regular freelancers, friends and the occasional bemused passerby to help organise, produce, set up, participate in and take down the parties, as and when they were needed. They had little idea of how one went about hiring personnel, sorting out the payroll, PAYE or any of the other myriad scary-sounding things that seemed to come with having employees.

Conducting interviews was a steep learning curve for Kim and David. Lisa Proto, one of Theme Traders' first employees, remembers going to the newly acquired Cricklewood warehouse – which had been grandly rechristened 'the Stadium' – and being asked to fill in an application for a PA's job in a tiny room full of costumes, with just enough room for an ironing board and a chair. She was then shown into the 'office', which was basically the warehouse reception, complete with solitary desk and single telephone.

David and Kim sat across from her, looking as uncertain as she was.

"Do you really want this job?" Kim asked in her usual forthright manner, "because you'll have to work really long hours, it's not very glamorous and you'll probably have to do lots of lugging about and other stuff we're not completely sure of yet, but which won't be glamorous either."

If Kim was trying to sell the job, she wasn't doing very well. In fact, the picture she painted was rather bleak. Furthermore, Lisa was starting to get the impression that neither Kim nor David were very clear on what her role would actually be. All they seemed to be interested in was a reassurance that if she worked for them, she'd be up for doing more or less anything at all, which luckily she was. As Lisa wandered out onto edgy, traffic-congested Cricklewood Broadway, with its mishmash of Asian greengrocers, bingo halls and greasy spoon cafes, she still couldn't quite get to grips with what had just happened. She'd been for a job interview at a company called Theme Traders, but what exactly was the job? And who the hell were Theme Traders?

Later that day, Lisa received a phone call from Kim.

"You've got the job!"

"Great. When do I start?"

"Tomorrow."

As Lisa was to find out, once Kim and David decide on something, they don't hang about.

Even as the fledgling Theme Traders grew, the Jamillys interviewing technique didn't get much more sophisticated. They tended to hire according to gut feeling rather than ticking off a list of criteria. And typically, each had very different interviewing styles.

Caroline Tyrrell-Evans applied to join Theme Traders after spotting an ad in the *Guardian*. Event management sounded rather exciting, she decided. Rather than send a normal, boring CV, she posted hers in a blue folder so that it would stand out, not realising that at Theme Traders, every file goes into some sort of blue folder. Delighted to be offered an interview she was taken aback when, having been shown into a room decorated entirely in blue and orange, a somewhat wild-haired woman stormed into the room, kicked the door shut and began to fire questions at her.

"What would you do for a Western party?"

Doing her best not to look nonplussed, Caroline plunged into a complicated response during which she deconstructed the differences between East and West, not noticing the look of growing incredulity on Kim's face. Finally the penny dropped. She meant a Wild West party. Doh! Kim's next question didn't exactly put her at her ease either. "Do you cry easily?"

Caroline started hearing the faint chimes of distant alarm bells ringing. If someone asks you at interview whether you're a crybaby, it can only mean one thing – the job they're offering is the kind of job that might just make a person cry. Kim's last question was even more tricky.

"Can you start next week?"

"Er, no, I have to work out my contract at the place where I'm temping."

Kim, who, as we've seen, doesn't see the point in waiting once she's made her mind up about something, was outraged.

"Why apply for a job if you can't start right now?" she wanted to know. Luckily, she calmed down enough to agree to a delayed start and within a few weeks, Caroline had joined TT as a trainee project manager.

Kim had already realised that working in the fledgling events industry was not going to be a job for those of a sensitive disposition. Employees would be expected to hold their own, pitching to a boardroom full of exacting businessmen. They'd

Kim's crying criteria

"I've had people who've found the job impossible and they come in crying their eyes out and I think, 'you're not going to last two minutes in this industry'. Little things like me calling something they've done 'stupid' in the heat of the moment (which I do to everyone, especially myself) make them cry. I'm sure if I was a better person I'd throw my arms around them and say 'don't cry', but my attitude is 'things like this happen – deal with it.' At one point it got to the stage where I was making so many people cry, I'd actually say in interviews 'do you cry easily?' because in this business people will try to push you around if you let them, and you have to be able to stand up to them. There used to be one girl who worked here and I used to see her pacing around outside my office before she came in and I'd think 'If she has to walk up and down for ten minutes just to get up the nerve to see me, what does she do when she runs into trouble on a job?'. If they can't deal with me being honest with them, they don't stand a chance of being able to deal with bullying clients. It's better to find out right at the start."

have to negotiate with performers, craftsmen, electricians and hauliers, often under the most pressurised conditions. They'd have to calm stressed out clients and take the flak when things went wrong. Plus they'd have to deal with Kim herself, known for speaking her mind no matter what. It was no place for fragile egos.

David, on the other hand, was a different kettle of fish entirely when it came to interviewing – laid back and quiet to the point where potential employees often didn't actually realise he was the boss.

Becky Handley was one candidate who was subjected to a David-style interview. After getting on the wrong train and ending up in St Albans, Becky wasn't optimistic about her chances of success when she finally pitched up in Cricklewood over an hour late, but David (or DJ as he soon became known to his staff) didn't seem to mind. He ambled in, shook her hand and asked her about her IT skills, at which Becky launched into an impressive spiel about all the databases she'd worked with.

David looked at her blankly.

"Crikey. But what I really meant was, can you type a letter?"

"Yes."

David's relief was obvious.

"Great. How about starting on Monday?"

Former TT employee, Alexandra Munro, remembers her interview as 'hilarious'. After passing the 'crying' test, Kim clearly decided Alex was the one for the job and summoned David downstairs, whereupon there ensued a big – and very loud – argument as to whether or not the company really needed an extra member of staff. As Alex sat in the interview room/broom cupboard pretending to be utterly absorbed in her train timetable, she tried to block out the raised voices outside the door. Having no idea David and Kim were siblings, she couldn't help thinking this a very odd way of managing a company. Eventually Kim won out and Alex, after overcoming a brief internal tussle over the wisdom of joining what was clearly a rather unorthodox business set-up, went on to discover that her new bosses were brother and sister and arguing was part of their creative process.

Kim's top 4 interview questions:

- Will you say yes to anything we ask you to do?
- Are you prepared to give up any semblance of a social life?
- How likely are you to burst into tears?
- Can you start today?

As David and Kim began hiring more staff and Theme Traders went from being a pair of siblings squabbling at a dining table to a proper, grown up company with letter-headed paper, premises and its own coffee maker, it became clear that it would need a basic structure.

Never having run a company before, and having no template for a successful events management company to follow, David and Kim made it up as they went along. Neither of them had ever been keen on hierarchical structures, with both in different ways having problems with authority, so at first they went for a communal type of management which was great – in theory.

The thing about theories though, is that they don't always translate into reality. What David and Kim soon realised that was management by committee was a) confusing, b) time consuming and c) completely unworkable. While everyone wanted a say in the decision-making process, they weren't prepared to also take a share of the responsibility.

David, reluctant to let go of his utopian ideals, held meetings where he encouraged puzzled staff members to lie on the floor and listen to Baz Lurhmann, hoping to engender some sense of team spirit and empowerment. What it actually did, unsurprisingly, was make people even more confused.

A lot of time was lost trying to work out who was responsible for what and who had the final say. An awful lot more time was lost trying to work out the hidden messages in Baz Luhrmann music.

Eventually it became clear that running a company as a complete democracy was not going to work. Gradually a structure emerged whereby David and Kim each had their own team working for them and answering to them. Later, as they took on more staff, sub-teams would also emerge with other people running the different departments of the business, like props and day-to-day operations (loading, shifting, organising). A projects team and four deputy directors were also created. But in the beginning it was all down to David and Kim.

For two people who'd spent twenty years happily banking their pay-checks and leaving the decisions up to someone else, becoming Boss was a steep learning curve. Gradually though they learned how to manage the staff they had, and crucially, how to recognise the right qualities at interview stage.

Once they knew what they were looking for, it was easier to build up a team of loyal, talented people willing to work insane hours. Over the years they went from 2 to 10 to an all-time high of 60 full time members of staff.

What to look for in a budding event organiser

- The ability to communicate with people – and to know when to listen.
- A passion for parties.
- Troubleshooting skills – coping as and when things go wrong.
- The ability to be spontaneous and adapt to a set of circumstances that may end up bearing little resemblance to an original brief.
- Someone who doesn't crumble under pressure.
- A willingness to do whatever is required, whether or not it falls out of the official job description.
- An awareness that there *is* no job description.
- Someone who's prepared to work long hours. Very long hours.
- An attention to detail.
- A team player.

But while Kim and David gradually became more accustomed to taking on staff, adapting to being bosses of a rapidly expanding business took more getting used to. Just as their interview techniques were wildly different, so too were the siblings' styles of management *(of which more later)*, with the always blunt and forthright Kim causing the more sensitive souls to burst into tears, and the quieter, more reflective David frequently mopping them up.

Kim readily admits she can be a demanding boss. "David's much nicer to people. He's much more of a person's person,"

Natalie Kiley (project manager):

"Kim is the most straightforward person I've ever met in my life. She's willing to say exactly what she thinks. When I first started I was absolutely petrified, although we're great friends now. She's absolutely the most un-two-faced person I know. She'll tell you straight down the line. David is more diplomatic."

Cat Sterry (props manager):

"There are different ways of talking to Kim and David, and it helps to understand them. With Kim you NEVER use the word 'no'. If Theme Traders is being asked to make something in 24 hours which really should take a week, you say 'yes, I can do that. But you might have to compromise on some of the details. Oh, and you'll have to pay the staff masses of overtime.'"

she says quite happily. "He's interested in whether people are satisfied and what their motives are for working here. I'm much more interested in 'let's get it done'. I'm much more brash."

Anyone coming to work for Theme Traders thinking event managing was all about wafting around a star-studded event with a giant clipboard tying bows around pillars was very rapidly put straight. Although by nature creative types, Kim and David nevertheless saw themselves principally as traders, just as it said on the tin. To their minds, the party industry was all about buying and selling – the client was buying their services, they were selling their expertise, ideas, props and costumes. Their staff – nearly all women – didn't just have to come up with whacky ideas for entertaining, they also had to be ready to stand up and sell. "These girls have to go into a City bank, say, and talk creatively with a boardroom full of men and then put a price on it, a realistic price," says Kim. "They have to know what they're talking about."

How Kim teaches her staff to sell:

- I don't let them answer the phone for about a year. If they pick up the phone and a client says they want to hire 6 cushions for a party, a new girl would say 'oh yes, that's 6 cushions at £25 each'. But what's the client having? A party. How big is the party? Is he spending £50, £1000, £40,000. It might be a big corporate event where there are loads more opportunities for us, but unless you have the confidence to ask the questions, you'll never find out.
- Never say 'no'. If someone rings and asks if we have a prop of a huge clock, I won't say 'no', I'll ask them what they want a big clock for. 'Well, we're having an event and we want a big clock with a stick of dynamite behind it to symbolise a ticking bomb' they might say. So we're not talking about a clock at all – we're talking about a time bomb. Can we make one of those. Yes. Again it's about communicating and asking the right questions.
- Be direct and straightforward. The other day I rang a big retailer where we have an account to buy

some glassware. She said 'your account is closed'.
I said 'If it's closed it's because we always pay it
off as we go. Can you reopen it please'. She said
'no, you have to open a new one and fill in all the
details again.' I said 'Can I just ask you something?
You're a retailer and I want to buy something from
you. Is there a problem with that?' 'No'. 'Then why
are you making it so difficult for me?' That's one
account they've lost because someone at the end of
the phone was more interested in form filling than
keeping a customer.

- Project confidence. If you're going to a meeting,
  always do your homework. Find out in advance as
  much about the person you're meeting as possible,
  through Google or other means. Not so that you
  come across as a mad stalker, but so you understand
  the context in which they operate.

In addition to knowing how to sell, all staff members were also expected to muck in with whatever needed doing, whether that was lifting, loading, rigging, performing, or painstakingly hand-sewing costumes.

It helped morale that Kim and David were also working at the same range of odd jobs as their staff. There was literally nothing the two bosses considered beneath them. Accountant, John O'Connor remembers coming to meet David for the first time at Oaklands Road, dressed in his most impressive suit, and finding the t-shirt clad company director whipping a vacuum cleaner around the reception area to show the cleaner how it worked.

This being the pre-health and safety days, there was no limit on the number of hours you could work and David frequently clocked up 48-hour shifts, making sure he was the first one to arrive and the last to leave – an attitude that couldn't help rubbing off on those around him.

Bernard O'Neill (businessman, long-time friend and occasional helper-out):

"I remember working with David at the Porchester one night. We finished about 2am and I thought 'phew, now we can go home'. Not a chance. We went on to two more venues to help de-rig. Then at 4am we got to this last venue and there were hundreds of heavy poles that needed shifting. I'd had it and refused to budge, but when you see David jump down and get stuck in without even stopping to think about it, you just have to help him. His determination and unfaltering willingness to do whatever needs to be done are inspiring."

Glamorous it certainly wasn't, but then neither could working at Theme Traders ever be described as dull. Plus the ridiculously antisocial hours – Becky recalls at least one December when she didn't see or talk to anyone outside of work the whole month – meant staff developed extremely close bonds, and there were lots of impromptu social get-togethers (leading to at least eleven TT marriages over the years and a clutch of TT babies). In fact the TT parties became legendary.

3 do's and don'ts of workplace parties

- DO play music, even if you're having the party in the office and have to play it on computers. It's invaluable in changing the mood from work to fun.
- DON'T stand around a group of desks as that physical barrier inhibits social interaction.
- DO play team games to relax people and remind them of the bonds they have in common.

Simeon Scott (former TT staff member, operations):

"The greatest thing about working at Theme Traders is the vibe. I work with my best friends, I work with great people, we have a laugh every second. We finish work, play football, go to the pub. This place is never boring."

the triumph of theming

With its newly acquired staff, Theme Traders in Cricklewood picked up more or less exactly where David and Kim in the mezzanine had left off. It was the early nineties – the age of rave culture, Girl Power, and fortuitously enough, the themed party. Suddenly everybody wanted to lose themselves in the fantasy and escapism of Hollywood or the Wild West or Outer Space. And David and Kim, raised at Laurence Corner, with its uniforms and fancy dress and opportunities to become someone else, were right there at the start.

For David – a self-confessed history geek – the revival of interest in themed events provided a fascinating link to the past and he began researching the timeline of theming, starting way back in the first century with the Roman emperor Domitian.

However, the history of theming through the ages has mostly been about festivals and commemoration of events rather than sheer flight of fancy. Where a party is held at a certain time or place every year to celebrate something that happened, people will often wear costumes in keeping with the original time and occasion and perform rituals, using specific props. For example,

Lerwick in the Shetland Isles hosts the Up-Helly-Aa every January where locals (and the more enthusiastic of the thousands of visitors who throng to the island every year) dress as Vikings and rampage happily through the streets, brandishing burning torches before setting fire to the wooden Viking ship they've spent the entire year constructing. After that the night is one long party, leaving the freezing streets heaped with drunken casualties the morning after. The Mexican Day of the Dead or All Souls Day is another cheerily themed festival where people honour their dead with toys and puppets painted like skeletons, and eat bread shaped like bones.

But though there has long been a history of dressing up for specific events, fantasy themed parties, in the style of Domitian, where the costumes, décor, lighting, and even food reflect the theme of the event, didn't really take off properly until the 1980s. Which was very lucky for a certain brother and sister from Hampstead Garden Suburb.

Domitian's back to black party

Domitian (51–96 AD) is notorious for his cruelty and ruthlessness, but few are aware that he also threw the first recorded themed bash – his 'death party'. He invited all the Roman senators to dinner at his house. The invites, coming from someone who had already executed senatorial opponents and had a habit of burning the genitals of those who got on his nerves, did not spark universal delight. Instead, the Senators who made their way to the Emperor's house at the appointed hour were understandably wary. Their anxiety increased a hundred fold when they were ushered into the banqueting room and found it had been painted completely black. Not only that, but Domitian had kitted out the tables to match with black cloths, black crockery and black goblets. Each of the guests was assigned a naked, black-painted boy to serve them. When they were shown to their seats, their fears weren't exactly assuaged by the fact that each of the table settings had an individual black tombstone on it. The food, when it arrived, was of the funereal kind and Domitian made a suitably sombre speech. When the senators made it to the end of the evening and back to their own homes without being disembowelled, their relief knew no bounds, but at 3am each was woken by a spine-chilling knock on the door. *Oh my God, here it comes*… was what passed through their heads (or the Latin equivalent). Trembling, they drew back the door to find, not the armed guard they'd been dreading or indeed the Grim Reaper himself, but the servant boy who'd served them at dinner, bearing the tombstone which turned out to be of solid silver and was a gift from the emperor, as was the boy himself, a life-long servant. Talk about the ultimate party bag… Domitian was no fool, he realised by throwing a party and showering his guests with generous gifts, he could buy their loyalty, but by theming it as cleverly as he did, he could also scare them into submission. Shame he didn't use the same strategy on his wife, who had him assassinated on 18 September 96 (AD).

In the beginning, the newly established Theme Traders operated a 'suck it and see' policy towards the whole question of theming. They'd already mastered the tried and tested fairground party, and to that they'd added a few staple themes like the Round the World Cruise or the Wild West party. In conjunction with legendary event manager, Mel Atkins of Finishing Touch, they started putting on Victorian-themed Christmas parties. Hiring the Connaught Rooms in London's Covent Garden for a set period over Christmas and booking in groups of companies on each night willing to shell out for their employees' Christmas bash, they'd recreate Victorian London with Dickensian painted backdrops and performers in Victorian dress. David would be in his straw boater and Victorian waistcoat, while Kim was running around briefing musicians, hawkers and magic acts.

For a few years, the Victorian parties were wildly successful, but as the public appetite for theming grew more sophisticated, it became obvious it was time to move on. This was a pattern, David and Kim were to become very used to over the coming two decades, as themes went in and out of fashion, and they were expected to stay constantly one step ahead of the trends and one leap of the imagination ahead of the punters.

As the nineties wore on, the themes got grander and more extravagant. Corporate clients caught onto the fact that having all the staff come to the annual knees-up dressed as superheroes or aliens, or all in red and white or neon or gold, not only gave everyone a talking point and a laugh, it actually bonded them as a team – one of the holy grails of the corporate world. The spend per head crept up as employers realised the subtle propaganda value of throwing a big themed bash.

Plus, of course, there was the inevitable one-upmanship. If one company threw a wild west party with twenty girls dressed in leather bikinis pouring tequila shots from holsters slung over their bare, bronzed shoulders, their nearest rival would have to go one better – an underwater party complete with seaweed tunnel, live lobsters and a brace of singing mermaids.

Prohibition, Rock n' Roll, Old London (anything from Dickens to Sherlock Holmes) were all popular. Film-based themes like James Bond, which gave the men a chance to be suave but conservative in dark tuxedos and the women a chance to be as risqué as they dared, were always in demand. The parties grew more involved – a Western party could have shootouts, rodeo bulls and waiters dressed as cowboys. Props could include the hangman's gallows and noose, or a Wells Fargo Stage Coach. The whole party set would be the mainstreet of a Wild West town complete with saloon and jail. There'd also be gambling, saloon girls and barn dancing.

A Prohibition party might involve entering through a dimly lit warehouse, the street littered with oil barrels, trashcans and old bicycles. Guests would pass through a set of metal speakeasy doors manned by heavies with violin cases, and then out into an opulently decorated nightclub, draped in velvet with a polished oak bar. Mingling with the invited guests would be gangsters' molls, gamblers, mobsters – and there might even be a mock police raid, in which the MD of the company would be marched off in handcuffs.

For each themed event they organised, Theme Traders built new props, made new table centres, painted new backdrops. There were costumes, invitations, performers, customised lights, etc. and these were all added to the company's steadily accumulating stock. Soon they'd outgrow the initial premises on Oaklands Road, Cricklewood and set themselves another target – to acquire a second set of warehouses on the same road known as Turpins Yard.

After that they bought premises to house the bulkier, less-used items further afield – a 100 acre farm in Leighton Buzzard where land was cheaper but transport links with London still excellent.

The initial, crudely drawn themes gave way to more conceptual, sophisticated ones. Theme Traders took on more project managers to originate, sell and manage the concepts and more prop-makers to see that vision through.

One of the hardest-learned skills for the project managers was to match the client to the theme, tailoring their own flights of fantasy to fit with the personality and expectations (not to mention the budget) of the person actually paying for the party. For a well-known socialite and philanthropist's 50th birthday bash, the theme chosen was 'women throughout history' and the party included tableaux of performers dressed as Cleopatra, the Goddess Diana, Mrs Pankhurst and Queen Victoria. The party was a great success, principally because the theme so clearly reflected the personality and interests of the hostess.

Accidental theming

Usually the themes are suggested by the project managers or the clients, or a combination of both but occasionally, they came about in a more inadvertent way, as with the Green Party. No, this was not anything to do with the environmentally-conscious political party of the same name, but the outcome of a private housewarming party Theme Traders was asked to organise for a client called Chris Tully. Chris was justifiably proud of the new eight-bedroom pile he'd just built in Hertfordshire and wanted to show it off to all his mates. As it was October, the idea was that the party would have a horror-slash-Halloween type theme. During the days immediately preceding the party, a marquee was erected in the grounds and much care taken to get every detail just right.

"Haven't you got anything we can put in the pool to liven it up?" Chris asked project manager Natalie at the eleventh hour, on the day before the party. Natalie glanced at the pristine outdoor swimming pool.

"I think we might have an outsize crocodile somewhere in the storeroom," she mused. "That'd look cool, as it's hollow so it will sink to the bottom and make an interesting feature."

The crocodile was duly brought over and unceremoniously tossed in the water where, true to form, it lurked menacingly on the bottom of the pool.

"Perfect," was the verdict.

The next morning, Natalie arrived at work to find a panic stricken message on her answering machine.

"Er, Natalie, it's Chris. Can you give me a ring? It's rather urgent. My f*****g swimming pool is bright green!"

Sure enough, when Natalie raced round to the house, she found the chlorine in the water had clearly reacted with the paint on the crocodile and turned the normally clear blue pool a bright, luminous lime colour.

It was too late to drain the pool. There was only one solution.

"We'll make it a green party," was Natalie's inspired response. There was just enough time to tweak the rest of the party to marry the two themes of Green and Horror before the guests started arriving.

> Two days later, an enormous bouquet of flowers arrived on Natalie's desk in Cricklewood. Nestling inside was a note from Chris. "Best party ever. Don't worry about the pool – it's gone down in history."

When David and Kim first started out in the party industry, theming as a business concept didn't exist (in fact they'd had to write to a university to find out whether or not it was spelled with a second 'e' after the 'm'), but during the nineties, other newly formed companies tried to jump on the event management bandwagon and lay on themed events of their own. The advantage Theme Traders had was that, being around from the beginning and having already accumulated so much party paraphernalia, they were able to see the bigger picture and stay one step ahead.

The themes kept getting bigger. Theme Traders was asked to do an Iron Maiden Party to celebrate the launch of the band's latest record and came up with the theme of Hollywood with a horror twist. They mocked up a Soho street and had Marilyn Monroe and Charlie Chaplin look-alikes with half their faces rotting away. Good taste it wasn't, but then it *was* Iron Maiden. The pièce-de-résistance was an electric chair that lit up whenever anyone sat on it, which was quite unfortunate for the couple who decided to stage a furtive erotic encounter on it. The company went on to do other Iron Maiden events, each more debauched than the last. One featured a snake charmer and a rat catcher. Unfortunately Kim, in her enthusiasm, had forgotten that snakes eat rats, so that whenever people touched the rats, and then went to pet the snake the poor creature went completely barmy – much to the consternation of its owner, who had it wrapped around her neck at the time.

The hairiest Iron Maiden moment came when the mud wrestlers, who'd been booked failed to show up, so Kim, in true Kim style, rustled up a pair of off-duty lifeguards from the hotel where the event was taking place. At the very last minute, when everything was in place, the mud wrestlers decided to roll up after all. They were big. And, when they discovered they'd been replaced, they were angry. Big and angry is not a great combination but Kim, to whom a promise is sacrosanct, refused to back down. "If you want to be taken seriously, you honour your commitments," she lectured the two towering hulks sternly.

One Iron Maiden party featured themed games to match each track on the new album, one incorporating a specially-built confession chamber complete with transvestite vicar being birched by a scantily clad girl. The 'vicar' later professed to being shocked at some of the confessions from the party guests. During the party a journalist who ventured outside the official area was bitten by a guard dog. Luckily Iron Maiden got all guests to sign an indemnity form before attending.

The act of theming, it seemed, immediately introduced a dimension of anarchy and of living and acting outside the normal rules, which was like gold dust when it came to parties going off with a bang.

The 7 deadly sins party

A wealthy client contacted Theme Traders about organising a birthday party at her palatial home in Lausanne, Geneva. Over a fantastic lunch in her exquisite dining room, she told Becky and Natalie, who'd flown in for the day, she'd decided on a 7 Deadly Sins theme. After much discussion the girls came up with a host of different acts including a sword swallower to illustrate Gluttony and a man lying on a bed of nails to illustrate Sloth. There would also be trapeze artists and burlesque strippers. Coordinating scores of specialist acts to travel from all over Europe is no mean feat, particularly when their props include swords and flammable liquid. The sword swallower had to drive because he wasn't allowed to take his swords on a plane and the flammable liquid for the fire grinders had to be sourced in Switzerland at the very last minute. When it finally arrived, with two hours to spare, it hadn't been mixed to the right proportions and ended up going everywhere except where it was supposed to go. The trapeze artists required a large, very tall marquee, but when the time came to rig it up, it was discovered the client's garden, which had originally been earmarked for the party, sloped too much and, rather than risk the performers swinging from a precariously teetering scaffolding, an alternative site close to the lake had to be hastily arranged. Then at the eleventh hour, there was a panic when it was discovered that somebody had forgotten to pack the table legs for the Casino tables. The flustered team rang around the whole of Switzerland searching for replacements with no joy before David eventually flew someone out from England with a suitcase crammed with table legs. Despite all the complications, the party was sinfully enjoyable. Of course, with a setting like that and enough money thrown at it, chances are it was always going to be more impressive than your average bash at the local cricket club, but the unusual and slightly risqué theme added an extra layer of experience and all the guests left knowing they'd been part of something truly unique.

David's top 10 tips for DIY theming on a budget:

- DO create pre-event anticipation with themed invitations.
- DO create a high impact entrance.
- DON'T waste money dressing floors and ceilings which are high budget/low return.
- DO work with (not in contrast to) existing architecture and features.
- DON'T go over the top – big is beautiful but beware of scale.
- DO remember that people make great props.
- DON'T underestimate candles and soft lighting.
- DO make the most of props and set pieces by centralising, dressing, texturing, painting and lighting.
- DO localise and focus impact points without diluting.
- DON'T forget – plants make a good sustainable statement.

As Theme Traders went from strength to strength in the industry, collecting staff members as they went, they also amassed a regular pool of performers willing to drop everything at a moment's notice to stand in as a walking currant bun or the back end of a circus horse.

Al Eve, a part-time actor, had first met Kim in 1987 when she was still working as a children's party entertainer and they both ended up face painting at the same event. Kim offered Al a lift home. Knowing what children's entertainers get paid Al gravitated to the tatty Volkswagen in the car park and was mortified when Kim unlocked the door of the new left-hand drive Merc. There are some benefits of being married to a diamond dealer, after all. Al's faux pas didn't get in the way of a friendship forming and after that, Kim would regularly ring Al when she and David needed an extra pair of hands for children's parties.

When Kim graduated to adult parties, once again she roped in her old mate to help her out. One of his first 'gigs' was as a fortune teller. Not knowing anything about it, Al went out and bought a 'how to' book on tea leaf reading and read it from cover to cover before the party, which was a corporate event at a big London hotel. He was shocked, not only by how good he turned out to be, but also how ready guests were to unburden themselves of their most intimate secrets, not always ones Al really wanted to know.

Over the years that followed the setting up of Theme Traders, Al did loads of parties for Kim and David, revelling in the fact that no two events were ever the same. These included the one for which he had to dress up as a giant profiterole, and the one where a well-known and much-loved (though not by Al) TV sports presenter thought it hilarious to lob balls at his back as he bent down to pick up coconuts from a coconut shy he was manning.

He was a gangster, a slave driver and once got attacked by two men inside a cage while dressed in drag (a night he prefers to draw a veil over). He did a party next door to Boy George's house in a very posh part of North London, where they decided to risk leaving all the party equipment in the van on the basis that crime didn't happen in leafy Hampstead. Wrong! All the instruments were stolen and David's prized magic set destroyed. Al also helped out in the early days at kids' parties, setting up treasure hunts at Althorpe House, home to Earl Spencer, and on one memorable occasion, in the revolving restaurant at the top of the Post Office Tower. And when there weren't any performer roles, he helped with the rigging and de-rigging and props delivery, often working alongside David, who would never ask the crew to do anything he wouldn't do himself.

One day he'd be delivering a rhino to Dunstable and the next he'd be picking up a giant gargoyle from Cambridge University or setting up the Mad Hatter's Tea Party in the gardens of Buckingham Palace.

After a sleepless night, she owned up to David about what had happened, offering to phone the client directly to 'fess up' and apologise.

"No need," David told her. "He's already been on the phone enthusing about the party and saying what a shame it was that nobody remembered to pick up the polaroids, but how lucky it was that you'd had the foresight to take extra photos."

Anna lived to photograph another day and learned one of the golden rules of events management: When things go wrong, you can always improvise.

The regular Theme Traders freelance crew didn't just consist of performers; there were also a fair smattering of friends, husbands and even the odd bemused passerby who got roped in to help out whenever it was needed.

Clifford Gee had first become friendly with David when he was working for Warner Brother's record group and David was playing in bands such as Jason and Gerome, which appeared on Top of the Pops under the expert management of Gary Davison. At the time Cliff was just nineteen, but he was the only one among the group of friends with a driving licence and his early memories are of driving gangs of very excitable people to and from from clubs like Samantha's in London's West End.

Even when Cliff climbed the corporate ladder, first setting up his own music management consultancy, managing record producers, and then his own cosmetics business, he remained close to both Jamilly siblings, and consequently was among those called upon when it was a case of all hands to the deck.

By day, Clifford might have been a highly respected businessman, but by night and at weekends he was often to be found lugging round scaffolding, putting away props in the

Right from the word go, David and Kim realised the value of building up a team of talented performers who knew the way the company worked and who wouldn't get sniffy about being asked to load and unload, plus make tea, mend costumes, drive vans and dress up in a variety of silly outfits.

Anna Lavado was another early recruit who became a regular stalwart in the Theme Traders squad. She first came across David and Kim when they were running the Christmas grotto at Whiteleys and was delighted to be given a job – even if it was as the back end of a reindeer.

The Jamillys quickly realised that anyone prepared to prance around a busy shopping centre in a boiling hot costume, clutching onto the nether regions of the person at the head was someone who was pretty much game for anything, and wasn't likely to throw a hissy fit or act the prima donna. Lisbon-born Anna got given more and more work. Again, it was the diversity of the jobs that kept her coming back for more.

One night she might be told to dress up as a giant pineapple, her pockets stuffed with chocolates, which the increasingly drunken guests were encouraged to skewer through the fabric of the costume (thanks for that idea, Kim). Then the next night she might hang out with Sting and his wife Trudie Styler. One of her regular duties came to be running the Sepia Photo booth at parties where guests could dress up in Victorian costumes and have their photos taken with a big old fashioned box camera (actually a Polaroid camera in disguise) and then instantly printed up in sepia tones. This was always a big hit and became a regular fixture at Theme Traders parties.

Anna had only one disaster in her long and illustrious career as a party photographer. It was during a private party at an exclusive advertising agency, which had a James Bond theme. She was playing the part of the female photographer from Dr No. "Come on," she cajoled the guests, "give me your best Bond-style poses." Everyone threw themselves into the swing of it, spending ages getting their poses exactly right and not noticing that the photographer's smile was becoming more and more fixed. Unbeknownst to the guests, each time Anna took a photo, it was coming out completely black. Whether it was a fault with the film or the camera, she had no idea. All she knew was that after she had got the guests to pose and then ripped off the picture backing as usual and waited… and waited… no image was appearing on the photo paper. All the photos were totally useless.

Anna hid her rising panic as she airily assured the guests their photos would be ready later. In the meantime, she suggested, why didn't she take a few photos on her mobile phone as well, which she could send on to them afterwards. Later, while the guests were tucking into their meal and her shift was over, she slung the box of ruined polaroids into her car and sped off.

Anna Lavado's weirdest party

"I was asked to do a job for Theme Traders at a weekend event in a big hotel. As it was Halloween, the theme was to be horror. The party on the Saturday night was a big success, but then Kim had the bright idea of making me the centrepiece for the breakfast table the next morning.

'You can be a dead head!' she told me excitedly.

It's fair to say my enthusiasm was slightly less than hers.

'Pardon?' I asked, hoping I'd misheard.

'We've got a long table with a hole in the middle and you'll be sitting on a stool underneath with your head

through a silver platter, which will be covering up the hole. We'll make you up with green face-paint to look like your skin is rotting. Genius, hey?'

'Genius' wasn't quite the word that was running through my head at 7am the next morning as I assumed my position under the table. I'd already been up for hours while my skin was painted sickly green, and my lips a disgusting purply shade of black. An itchy, long, black wig covered my head, my face was draped with cobwebs and a crowd of tiny fake spiders spilled out of my mouth. To be frank, I'd looked better.

When the guests arrived, to be greeted by the sight of a dead, mouldering head alongside their breakfast spread, reactions ranged from horrified to amused to unprintable. I had to listen to them all without changing expression. Many couldn't decide whether the head actually belonged to a dummy and one cheeky bugger, sitting alarmingly close to me, debated long and hard the merits of sticking his fork into my eye to check if I was real. I think he'd have discovered very quickly just how real I was if he'd tried anything of the kind.

Never did a breakfast drag quite so much. Two hours is an awfully long time to be hunched on a stool with spiders spilling out of your mouth, playing at being dead.

'Was it fun?' Kim asked me afterwards.

I glared at her, through eyes still swollen from the effects of the Dead Head make up, my neck still cricked after hours of holding it in one position.

I think she got the message, because I was never asked to revive that particular part again."

warehouse, rigging or drilling holes in the bottoms of candles to fit inside candelabra. When Theme Traders moved out of the garages and into the new premises in Cricklewood, it was Cliff who landed the job of transporting the not-quite-lifesize model of the Statue of Liberty along the street from the van.

"Whatever you do, don't damage the hand. It's fragile," yelled David, as Cliff teetered along under the weight of the unwieldy statue, his heart in his mouth every time he had to negotiate a tight corner or a particularly low-lying door jamb, wondering for the hundredth time, just how he'd ended up in this position.

If you came anywhere within the Jamillys' social orbit, it seemed you were fair game whenever Theme Traders put on a show. Gary Davison, an old schoolfriend of David's who later went on to manage one of David's numerous bands was one of many who got roped into helping out on his time off from his music business job.

Kim or David would ring with the address of a venue and he'd turn up to discover he was down to make the drinks or unload the vans or make sure the props were positioned correctly.

Gary Davison (childhood friend and music executive):

"I've served drinks to stern-looking people in army barracks round the back of Buckingham Palace and given up my Saturday to be an extra in a film shot at Oaklands Road. Loads of Kim and David's friends have helped out over the years. It's fun – and obviously we're cheap!"

The Jamillys' friends on the whole held down responsible, time-consuming jobs. Yet for some reason, many of them were willing to give up their precious free time to help out in the most menial, and often bizarre tasks. There was just something about the organised chaos of Theme Traders, and the unpredictability of it, plus the sense of loyalty Kim and David inspired that seemed to make giving up your Saturday night to go to some stranger's party dressed as a big, fluffy yellow chicken quite an irresistible proposition.

Right from the word go, David and Kim realised the value of building up a team of talented performers who knew the way the company worked and who wouldn't get sniffy about being asked to load and unload, plus make tea, mend costumes, drive vans and dress up in a variety of silly outfits.

Anna Lavado was another early recruit who became a regular stalwart in the Theme Traders squad. She first came across David and Kim when they were running the Christmas grotto at Whiteleys and was delighted to be given a job – even if it was as the back end of a reindeer.

The Jamillys quickly realised that anyone prepared to prance around a busy shopping centre in a boiling hot costume, clutching onto the nether regions of the person at the head was someone who was pretty much game for anything, and wasn't likely to throw a hissy fit or act the prima donna. Lisbon-born Anna got given more and more work. Again, it was the diversity of the jobs that kept her coming back for more.

One night she might be told to dress up as a giant pineapple, her pockets stuffed with chocolates, which the increasingly drunken guests were encouraged to skewer through the fabric of the costume (thanks for that idea, Kim). Then the next night she might hang out with Sting and his wife Trudie Styler. One of her regular duties came to be running the Sepia Photo booth at parties where guests could dress up in Victorian costumes and have their photos taken with a big old fashioned box camera (actually a Polaroid camera in disguise) and then instantly printed up in sepia tones. This was always a big hit and became a regular fixture at Theme Traders parties.

Anna had only one disaster in her long and illustrious career as a party photographer. It was during a private party at an exclusive advertising agency, which had a James Bond theme. She was playing the part of the female photographer from Dr No. "Come on," she cajoled the guests, "give me your best Bond-style poses." Everyone threw themselves into the swing of it, spending ages getting their poses exactly right and not noticing that the photographer's smile was becoming more and more fixed. Unbeknownst to the guests, each time Anna took a photo, it was coming out completely black. Whether it was a fault with the film or the camera, she had no idea. All she knew was that after she had got the guests to pose and then ripped off the picture backing as usual and waited… and waited… no image was appearing on the photo paper. All the photos were totally useless.

Anna hid her rising panic as she airily assured the guests their photos would be ready later. In the meantime, she suggested, why didn't she take a few photos on her mobile phone as well, which she could send on to them afterwards. Later, while the guests were tucking into their meal and her shift was over, she slung the box of ruined polaroids into her car and sped off.

Anna Lavado's weirdest party

"I was asked to do a job for Theme Traders at a weekend event in a big hotel. As it was Halloween, the theme was to be horror. The party on the Saturday night was a big success, but then Kim had the bright idea of making me the centrepiece for the breakfast table the next morning.

'You can be a dead head!' she told me excitedly.

It's fair to say my enthusiasm was slightly less than hers. 'Pardon?' I asked, hoping I'd misheard.

'We've got a long table with a hole in the middle and you'll be sitting on a stool underneath with your head through a silver platter, which will be covering up the hole. We'll make you up with green face-paint to look like your skin is rotting. Genius, hey?'

'Genius' wasn't quite the word that was running through my head at 7am the next morning as I assumed my position under the table. I'd already been up for hours while my skin was painted sickly green, and my lips a disgusting purply shade of black. An itchy, long, black wig covered my head, my face was draped with cobwebs and a crowd of tiny fake spiders spilled out of my mouth. To be frank, I'd looked better.

When the guests arrived, to be greeted by the sight of a dead, mouldering head alongside their breakfast spread, reactions ranged from horrified to amused to unprintable. I had to listen to them all without changing expression. Many couldn't decide whether the head actually belonged to a dummy and one cheeky bugger, sitting alarmingly close to me, debated long and hard the merits of sticking his fork into my eye to check if I was real. I think he'd have discovered very quickly just how real I was if he'd tried anything of the kind.

Never did a breakfast drag quite so much. Two hours is an awfully long time to be hunched on a stool with spiders spilling out of your mouth, playing at being dead.

'Was it fun?' Kim asked me afterwards.

I glared at her, through eyes still swollen from the effects of the Dead Head make up, my neck still cricked after hours of holding it in one position.

I think she got the message, because I was never asked to revive that particular part again."

After a sleepless night, she owned up to David about what had happened, offering to phone the client directly to 'fess up' and apologise.

"No need," David told her. "He's already been on the phone enthusing about the party and saying what a shame it was that nobody remembered to pick up the polaroids, but how lucky it was that you'd had the foresight to take extra photos."

Anna lived to photograph another day and learned one of the golden rules of events management: When things go wrong, you can always improvise.

The regular Theme Traders freelance crew didn't just consist of performers; there were also a fair smattering of friends, husbands and even the odd bemused passerby who got roped in to help out whenever it was needed.

Clifford Gee had first become friendly with David when he was working for Warner Brother's record group and David was playing in bands such as Jason and Gerome, which appeared on Top of the Pops under the expert management of Gary Davison. At the time Cliff was just nineteen, but he was the only one among the group of friends with a driving licence and his early memories are of driving gangs of very excitable people to and from from clubs like Samantha's in London's West End.

Even when Cliff climbed the corporate ladder, first setting up his own music management consultancy, managing record producers, and then his own cosmetics business, he remained close to both Jamilly siblings, and consequently was among those called upon when it was a case of all hands to the deck.

By day, Clifford might have been a highly respected businessman, but by night and at weekends he was often to be found lugging round scaffolding, putting away props in the

warehouse, rigging or drilling holes in the bottoms of candles to fit inside candelabra. When Theme Traders moved out of the garages and into the new premises in Cricklewood, it was Cliff who landed the job of transporting the not-quite-lifesize model of the Statue of Liberty along the street from the van.

"Whatever you do, don't damage the hand. It's fragile," yelled David, as Cliff teetered along under the weight of the unwieldy statue, his heart in his mouth every time he had to negotiate a tight corner or a particularly low-lying door jamb, wondering for the hundredth time, just how he'd ended up in this position.

If you came anywhere within the Jamillys' social orbit, it seemed you were fair game whenever Theme Traders put on a show. Gary Davison, an old schoolfriend of David's who later went on to manage one of David's numerous bands was one of many who got roped into helping out on his time off from his music business job.

Kim or David would ring with the address of a venue and he'd turn up to discover he was down to make the drinks or unload the vans or make sure the props were positioned correctly.

Gary Davison (childhood friend and music executive):

"I've served drinks to stern-looking people in army barracks round the back of Buckingham Palace and given up my Saturday to be an extra in a film shot at Oaklands Road. Loads of Kim and David's friends have helped out over the years. It's fun – and obviously we're cheap!"

The Jamillys' friends on the whole held down responsible, time-consuming jobs. Yet for some reason, many of them were willing to give up their precious free time to help out in the most menial, and often bizarre tasks. There was just something about the organised chaos of Theme Traders, and the unpredictability of it, plus the sense of loyalty Kim and David inspired that seemed to make giving up your Saturday night to go to some stranger's party dressed as a big, fluffy yellow chicken quite an irresistible proposition.

While organising the parties might have satisfied David and Kim's creative streaks, the prop hire was proving to be the bread and butter of the organisation. Big events came and went, but every day there was a steady stream of calls from people wanting to rent everything from a leopard-print chaise longue to a 9ft igloo. Other party organisers, television companies, corporate PRs organising a product launch all came calling whenever they were in need – there was no shortage of people looking for the weird, wonderful and slightly obscure. Often Theme Traders would already have exactly what they needed among its rows and rows of carefully warehoused stock. If not, they'd make it, knowing that whatever it was, they could always hire it out again.

There existed a universally held conception that prop-making was a specialist skill honed by years at art college, but ever since the Jamillys had knocked up those original fairground stalls in Kim's back garden, they'd realised two important things:

- Anyone can make virtually anything, as long as you break it down into small manageable parts.

- Prop-making is as much about vision as artistic training. You can teach the technical stuff, but you can't teach someone how to believe that anything is possible as long as you approach it logically or to think outside the box.

In the early days everyone had a go at making the props and the costumes and even painting the scenery, but as TT developed as a company, and naturally divided up into departments, a designated props team began to develop.

When Cat Sterry was asked as a child what she wanted to do when she grew up, she surprised her teachers by not aspiring to be a vet or an airline stewardess like the rest of her classmates, but to 'make monsters'. That somewhat eccentric vision never faded and unsurprisingly, after graduation, she naturally gravitated towards prop making as a career. In the mid 1990s, she found herself freelancing for a film prop studio based down the road from Theme Traders in Turpins Yard (the series of warehouses which Theme Traders would later buy). Watching the Theme Traders vans driving up and down the road made her curious about just what was going on at the mysterious Stadium a block up, so she sauntered up one lunchtime to find out.

Immediately she was struck by the proliferation of weird and whacky props everywhere she looked and decided on the spot she'd like to work there. But though David was happy to take her on, there was one delicate sticking point. Money.

"I want £10 an hour," she insisted (this was the 1990s, remember.)

"We can only offer you half that," was David's response. "All our stuff's seen in the dark anyway, so we don't need a proper prop maker."

It's a reply which Cat still treasures to this day.

Cat went away and forgot all about the company until a couple of years later, when she saw they were advertising for a full-time prop maker. Though she lost out on that job to someone else, she was offered a full-time, freelance contract, quickly proving so indispensable that she now runs the props workshop and is one of the company's deputy directors (earning considerably more than £10 an hour).

Working in props is one of those jobs where each day is totally different from the last and Cat has lost count of the unusual and downright bizarre things she's been asked to make over the years – from a giant pig, 6ft long by 5ft high, to an 8ft high condom for World Aids Day.

Although she already had a props background, making props for film and theatre is very different to parties, where things have to be transported long distances and assembled and disassembled very quickly.

David:

"Our props are one-offs. They're always distinctive, which is bad in a way because guests always want to take them home as unofficial mementos, but good because they're so easily identifiable. I remember turning up at 2.30am one night to de-rig after an event in the centre of London. As I was approaching the venue, I passed a guy wandering down the deserted road, clasping a giant 6ft high silver boot. 'Oi!' I yelled, winding the car window down, 'I rather think that's mine!'"

Sometimes working in the isolation of the high-ceilinged workshop, you can lose sight of how something will look when it's in situ. Cat remembers slaving for hours over a one metre diameter globe. It was done in two halves which were then fibre-glassed together. She'd just finished filling and sanding the join when a horrible thought occurred. Would it fit through the workshop door? The short answer was no. The globe had to be ground in half again, and then re-fitted together in the loading bay.

Another time, Cat was on holiday when she received a panicky call from her assistant, Nina. As it was quarter to one in the morning, Cat was fairly sure the news wasn't going to be good.

"I can't get the dinosaur's head through the door."

Nina had been working for days on a model of a giant T Rex head for fashion designer Matthew Williamson's window displays at his Bruton Street store. It had been finished, polished and perfected and the guys were there to wrap it up, before the mistake had been realised. And it was due in the shop the following morning!

"You're going to have to cut it."

Were ever seven words more unwelcome? Nina, who had her coat and bag on ready to leave, had to get back into her overalls and grab the polystyrene cutter – basically a cheese wire with an electric current. Then she had to cut her prize creation in half and glue it back together again in the loading bay. Nowadays, everyone who works in props has an invisible tattoo across the back of their hands: 86 centimetres – the width of the door.

Most of the props Theme Traders send off tend to be made from polystyrene, which is easy to carve and can then be finished off to look like marble or plaster or whatever effect the client wants.

One of Cat's more ambitious tasks was to make a lifesize model of Michelangelo's David statue. She had eight days to do it, which was enough time for the carving. However, then the client also stipulated a marble finish, tough enough to be weatherproof as they wanted the statue to stand outside. Now that was trickier. A finish like that would require five and a half out of the eight days for sanding, filling and painting. In the end it was a toss up – a perfect David, or a perfect marble finish? The client opted for the marble meaning that, while the master himself had laboured over his masterpiece for three long years, Cat had just over two days to knock out a passable imitation.

How to carve a 2 metre tall statue of Michelangelo's David in 2 and a half days:

- Don't make the mistake of using more than one person to do the carving to speed things up – you'll end up with a mismatch of styles and perspectives.
- Do NOT think of it as a whole figure or you'll run screaming from the room.
- Think about it instead as a series of shapes – a head is a ball-shape, the nose is a triangle shape.
- Once the basic shapes are there, start fine-tuning, but only one section at a time so it's not too daunting.
- Don't panic if you accidentally lop off a hand or an ear, the beauty of polystyrene is you can always glue it back on again.

Over the years, as materials became more sophisticated, Cat and her team were able to turn their hands to an increasingly diverse range of projects. Plastazote was a substance that revolutionised costume making – sheets of yoga-mat texture material that could be glued or heated together to make a great looking, lightweight structure. Gone were the days when some poor unfortunate wearing a giant cigarette costume would have to teeter around, under metres of thick upholstery foam covered in fabric. Plastazote made even spending the evening dressed up as a giant foot bearable. And as an added bonus, the costumes could always be 'borrowed' by the staff for special occasions, like when Cat and Lisa went to a black tie party at a garden centre dressed respectively as a strawberry and an apple.

Of course, there are the things that don't go to plan – the 30 cacti for one of Madonna's shows that were needed so urgently that everyone in the company had to put boiler suits over their smart outfits and take up a paintbrush; or the time they had to make four giant sharks, each representing a different country, to be shipped to Geneva, and Cat assumed that because the first shark's head only took her a couple of hours, they'd get the whole job done in two and a half days (cue some very, very tired prop-workers); or the time Oaklands Road flooded while Cat was on a training course and by the time she rushed back all her precious props were bobbing about in the water.

Over the years, as the party market fluctuated, props went on to become the nuts and bolts of Theme Traders. It now employs 5 full time staff and one on a permanent contract, as well as a big pool of freelancers who can be called upon when there's a rush job or at busy times like Christmas. As Cat eased into her role, she developed a very clear idea of what she was looking for in her staff:

- A creative eye (much more important than technical skill).
- Adaptability – like everyone in the company, prop makers might suddenly have to drop their tools and help load the van, or de-rig if the operations department is short staffed. Anyone who considers themselves too much of an artist to get their hands dirty won't last long.
- Lack of preconceptions – if you have set ideas of how something should be done or made, you're not going to be able to rush it through in half the time or change the dimensions at the last minute to suit the particular space or brief.

The moment Cat realised her job could be a lot worse:

"One time we were doing an amazing window display in Turkey with props and live performers. I was fitting the elaborate headdresses we'd made when I became aware of a gorgeous male model loitering expectantly in front of me, wearing only a g-string and a lot of body paint. 'Er, are you waiting for me?' I asked. Then, I noticed there was a woman kneeling behind him wielding a little pair of scissors. 'I won't be a moment,' she apologised. 'I'm just trimming his bum hair.' I've never complained about my own job since!"

CHAPTER NINE
the champagne years

From the moment Kim first put her hand up at the TV-am party meeting and said "I can do that", Theme Traders' philosophy had been 'never say no' and that mantra served them well throughout the nineties. Of course, it was wonderful do the huge, star-studded events, but if someone called asking to hire a chair for £30 or if another event planner wanted to use either their props or their expertise, they weren't about to turn them away. One time a woman rang by mistake thinking they were a furniture wholesaler and by the time she put the phone down Kim had sold her a job lot of high-backed, velvet-cushioned chairs made for a film set. That flexibility would serve them well in an industry that seemed to change direction just as fast as it grew.

One of the early signs that events were starting to be taken very seriously indeed was the opening up of landmark buildings for use as venues. Before the early nineties, parties were held in hotels or special function halls, but suddenly some of the best known buildings in London and other large cities were cottoning onto the fact that private parties were an excellent money spinner.

Madame Tussauds, HMS Belfast, Tower Bridge – all rented themselves out as backdrops for spectacular events, and once again David and Kim were in right at the start. The company's versatility proved its great strength. By offering themselves up as a supplier of lighting, props, scenery, they weren't limited to competing for one of the few prized party-organiser contracts; they were able to get involved in events organised by other people at any given level. When the Natural History Museum threw open its historic doors to party revellers, Theme Traders were one of its approved suppliers, their name on the list given to anyone organising an event in its atmospheric Gothic vaulted interior.

In this way, they forged links with other companies also feeling their way in the still youthful world of event management. Their early partners included a company called Fanfare 3000, run by Peter Richardson and Paul Baxter and Admirable Crichton, under the control of Johnny Roxburgh, one of the all-time great event managers.

It was through Roxburgh that they became involved with the 1995 Goldeneye film premier party, held at the Imperial War Museum to celebrate Pierce Brosnan's debut outing as James Bond. There the lines between fantasy and reality blurred as MI6 agents (well, actually 'resting' actors recruited through the *Stage*) mingled with the rich and famous, trying to recruit them to join the secret service.

As the mid-nineties boom continued, there was plenty of work to go around. The mood in the country was buoyant and conspicuous wealth had not yet gone out of style. Corporations wanted to be seen to be generous to their staff and their clients, and parties provided an instant showcase for a company's prosperity. When Krug Champagne wanted to celebrate a successful year's trading, Theme Traders threw a '20,000 Bubbles under the Sea' party, featuring one of their performers, Al Eve, dressed in gold swimming trunks and body paint as Neptune, King of the Sea. It was as if excess had come to be synonymous with success.

But the party which really illustrated the ebullient indulgence of the nineties was the London Stock Exchange Party in 1996. For Theme Traders this was a milestone event, not just because it was the biggest they'd ever organised completely autonomously, but also because, at £100,000 for the company's production fee alone, it was by far the most expensive to date.

The party was to celebrate the so-called Big Bang, when Stock Exchange technology shifted from old to new. The theme was the origins of the Stock Exchange, which wasn't nearly as dry as it sounds. Guests would enter through a dramatic time tunnel, with 16ft high banks of scenery ranging from an old London street scene complete with goats, chickens, straw and Victorian characters right the way through to a painted panorama of the modern London skyline. Inside the Stock Exchange itself the gel on the lights had been changed to blue. There were 20 production personnel, 20 lighting technicians and thirty actors, plus dozens of line managers. The whole thing was months in the planning and David even joined a gym to get fit enough to cope with the sudden pressure. There were endless meetings, endless logistical problems.

"Of course you'll have gone through all of this before…" the client would say confidently. David would nod, hoping it wasn't too obvious that just a few short years before, he'd been dressing up in a spaceman outfit to entertain twenty hyper children for £200 a time.

The London Stock Exchange Party went off with a, well, big bang. After the last guests had left and David walked into the room where the client representatives had gathered, still buzzing with adrenalin from the evening's events, there was a spontaneous round of applause. It seemed like everything Theme Traders did turned to gold, and that the party bubble, which began just a few years earlier, was going to keep on growing bigger and bigger...

By 1997, David and Kim were turning over £1m a year. While neither of them were totally sure what this meant to them personally or as a company, they knew that all those noughts must be pretty good. And people weren't showing any signs of growing tired of celebrating.

As the event management industry grew more mainstream, it started to lose its rough-around-the-edges image and become more tightly regulated. The first event management degree courses sprang up at universities, where students could learn the text-book approach to organising parties. Moves were made to centralise the industry, with the International Special Events Society (ISES), already established in America, setting up a UK branch in 1997.

At first Kim and David were excited by the new developments, thinking that professional accreditation and tighter regulations meant event management would have a more professional image and be taken more seriously. Kim even became one of the founder members of the British ISES branch, and David would go on to be Member of the Month in 2008. But like their father and grandfather before them, the Jamilly siblings were essentially mavericks, and being affiliated to a central authority didn't sit well with their more anarchic leanings. There were occasions where Theme Traders' forthright, upfront style clashed with the more bureaucratic central agency. Their choice to remain largely outside the umbrella group may have lost them some opportunities for building reciprocal links with other party planners, but it meant they retained their independence. And anyway, with the party business still booming, there was plenty of work to go round.

One side effect of the new professionalisation of the industry was the gradual tightening up of health and safety regulations. When Kim and David had started out, there were very few in the way of set rules governing the hours they or their staff could work, or the things they were allowed to do or what they had to wear on their heads, feet or knees while they did them. As more and more people came into the business, however, the first signs of the new bureaucracy (which would later flourish under the overprotective eye of the nanny state) began to appear, such as the so-called Ladder Rule whereby any ladder over 6ft was required to have two people holding it. "Hogwash", is Kim's predictable response.

Richard Lyons (Theme Traders' head of operations):

"Before Health and Safety kicked in, I remember working 52 hours straight. One time, I was driving a van behind DJ alongside a whole strip of roadworks on the A1 and suddenly noticed he was swerving and knocking all the cones over. Turned out he'd fallen asleep. Another time, when the company first bought Turpins Yard, I was cleaning out one of the upper warehouse spaces and I dropped a box of chemicals on the metal stairs and they started melting – more worryingly, so did my shoes! Mind you, I think it's all gone a bit crazy now. The new Health and Safety rules might have reduced the potential for accidents, but they've also seriously inhibited what we can do."

On the whole though, the mid to late nineties were buoyant years for the events industry, and the country as a whole. In 1997, Tony Blair swept to power in a landslide victory for Labour, after 18 years in the political wilderness. Suddenly there was a new optimism in the air, a sense that real change was about to happen. The world felt newer, younger, shinier. The fresh-faced, new prime minister celebrated his arrival in Downing Street with a series of celebrity-studded receptions, immediately dubbed the 'Cool Britannia' parties. Rock stars like Noel Gallagher, iconic artist Tracey Emin and young actors and performers such as Ralph Fiennes, Lenny Henry and Ben Elton, rubbed shoulders at these glittering occasions to demonstrate their support for the new order.

Suddenly parties were not just frivolous hedonistic events but powerful political tools. Theme Traders' phones were ringing off the hook. And of course, it wasn't just the new political landscape that gave events planners such a boost, but the growing anticipation, which began years in advance, that just over the horizon lurked what would surely be the biggest, wildest, most extravagant party of them all – the millennium.

Nobody had the remotest idea what 31 December 1999 would bring, having never experienced a millennium before. But in the late nineties speculation was rife that this would be the night to end all nights. And all around it there would be other commemorative events – a whole rich tapestry of social gatherings celebrating the end of one era and the start of another.

As if to warm up, the party industry was flexing its by now considerable muscle. There were themed events, corporate events, each more showy than the last. Global corporations thought nothing of flying thousands of staff in for one event. The average spend per head shot up from under £85 per head (the tax threshold for entertaining staff) to hundreds or even thousands, with the extra money being shaved off promotional budgets or staff training budgets.

Most of us wouldn't dream of spending more than a total of a few hundred quid on a party. Tops. A couple of crates of beer, a couple of mixed boxes of wine from Oddbins, some new compilation CDs, some baguettes and a few bowls of crudités and crisps. So the idea of spending £1000 or even £2000 per head on a single night seems unfathomable, but the big business parties of the late 20th century had no such psychological constraints. If you worked for Goldman Sachs you wanted to be able to say to your chum at Merrill Lynch, "Well, at our party we had X named band, and X brand of champagne" and then your chum at Merrill Lynch would have to outdo that. Where once companies would have employed an Abba tribute band, now they wanted the real thing. Massive global stars like James Brown were booked to play for a few hundred people at corporate events. There was Cristal champagne. Guests arrived by helicopter and left with goodie bags bulging with designer gifts.

David explains how to spend £2000 per head on a party

- If you think of the actual components of a party, what the money goes on – the most expensive thing you can do is to build a house from scratch. So, building a completely new structure would send the budget shooting up immediately.
- Even erecting a marquee is only as cheap as you want it to be. A marquee starts out as a

white tent, like any room starts out as bare white concrete walls. It's how you build up from there and the luxury you bring in that dictates the budget.

- Do you want a 'wow' element, like a canal going through the marquee, complete with real gondolas? It's possible.

- Do you bring the designer elements from Ikea or from Philippe Starck? That could raise the spend from £100 to £1000.

- In terms of design, we could bring in some Picassos or some cutting edge stuff designed for this occasion; we could bring in celebrities. We could pour the best champagne and serve only vintage wines and caviar. We could add layer upon layer of luxury, making the experience of sitting in that marquee or that basic room cost £100,000 or £200,000. It's not going to cost a lot more than that, unless we transport the room to Marrakesh – which has also been known.

All through the late nineties, the parties snowballed in terms of opulence, extravagance and sheer excess. And all the time in the back of everyone's head was this little voice promising 'you ain't seen nothing yet'. Because if this was what events were like already, surely the millennium would be even more out of this world, even more breathtaking? It would be the party to end all parties and everything that had preceded it would seem a mere shadow. The buzz built as people stopped being bothered about the waste or the unjustifiable extravagance. This was the one time in history when everyone was forgiven for putting enjoyment to the top of the agenda despite wars, famine and global poverty.

Billions were laid out on ambitious projects like the controversial Millennium Dome in Greenwich and the more universally acclaimed Millennium Wheel on the South Bank. The Millennium Bridge, a ribbon of twisted steel spanning the Thames in front of the newly opened Tate Modern art gallery, was already underway although it wouldn't actually open until June 2000 (and then close almost immediately afterwards as pedestrians complained its exaggerated swaying movement made them feel sick). Everywhere there were signs of expansion and expenditure, as cities and countries jostled to impress with increasingly extravagant displays of civic pride and prosperity.

Theme Traders continued to thrive, as did their bank balance. By the turn of the millennium they were turning over £2m a year and it seemed like nothing was going to hold them back.

They'd teamed up with Maurice Godden, one time butcher and Department of Trade and Industry small business advisor. Maurice knew lots of things about lots of subjects but the one thing he really, *really* understood was financial planning.

Under Maurice's guidance, David and Kim deftly boned and filleted their still largely raw event management business. He asked them scary sounding (but actually very fundamental) questions featuring terms like "bottom line" and "target-meeting". He got them to look honestly at where they wanted to see the business in five years time? Ten years? What was their policy on giving credit to clients (left up to Kim, nobody but NOBODY would ever get credit from Theme Traders, whereas David leant more towards allowing the bigger customers like the BBC some leeway in settling bills).

Profit-wise, the future was looking rosy. Already the media was predicting an unprecedented party season. London was planning the ultimate fireworks display, culminating in a fabulous river of fire sweeping dramatically down the Thames, and there were celebrations being talked about in every city, every village. Events managers took on more staff, universities churned out event management graduates by the truckload, local councils fretted about noise levels, road closures and laying on extra refuse collectors.

Everyone was on tenterhooks waiting for the explosion of special effects, revelry and unparalleled celebration that was lurking expectantly just around the corner, at the very tail end of 1999. And Theme Traders were perfectly positioned to take advantage of this brave new party world.

The countdown had begun.

CHAPTER TEN
the millennium and beyond

As party organisers, Kim and David of all people should have known that nothing ever goes quite to plan. The higher the expectations, the greater the potential for disappointment. With the stage all set for the biggest celebration of all time, and everyone on earth planning to party like it's 1999, the millennium was really always destined to be a damp squib. The truly shocking thing was just how much of a damp squib it was.

For a start, there was the date. With billions of people primed for countdown, you'd think someone would have worked out a global consensus for exactly which date the celebration should fall, but sadly, no such agreement was reached. According to purists, the 3rd millennium didn't start until 1 January 2001, which would put the millennium celebrations on 31 December 2000. But the world loves a round number and most people simply wouldn't countenance the millennium beginning on anything other than 1 January 2000. Already the seeds of fragmentation were sown.

The hype surrounding the transition of the 20th century into the 21st was proven to be just that – hype. In some cases that wasn't a bad thing – the much heralded Millennium Bug where computer systems running all the world's major institutions were predicted to crash, bringing chaos and anarchy, never arrived. Nostradamus' catastrophic predictions of death and destruction didn't materialise. Survivalists who hunkered down in specially built bunkers with enough supplies to see them through the End of the World as We Know It, emerged weeks later to find very little had actually changed.

But what of the parties – the huge, never-to-be-forgotten extravaganzas we'd all be talking about for generations to come? These too proved to be largely products of a fevered, collective imagination.

Pubs and clubs hiked their prices so much that most people didn't bother. Alarmed by warnings of huge crowds and overpriced and over-burdened taxi services, many decided to stay home and watch the celebrations on the telly. Some unlucky event managers, who'd been staffing up in anticipation of their busiest season ever, were left largely twiddling their thumbs.

If David and Kim were disappointed by the underwhelming start to the new millennium, they were not altogether surprised. It's often the case that the greater the expectations, the bigger the contingency plan needs to be, and throughout the run-up to December 1999, they'd continued plugging away at the props business and accepting the smaller jobs, rather than pinning all their hopes and resources on the big spectaculars that never materialised. Over the following months, they quietly consolidated their position as one of the biggest and certainly the most comprehensive events company in the marketplace. They appeared on TV, with both giving live interviews for the Money Channel, and had a full-page devoted to their burgeoning business in *The Times*.

In the wider events world, however, the situation was less secure. Though the party business picked up over the year that followed the limping in of the new millennium, with some of the biggest and brashest of the corporate parties taking place over those months, it was to be a short-lived revival. The years following the anticlimax of the 2000 millennium saw three events in quick succession that would effectively burst the fragile bubble of the newly established events industry – the crashing of the dot-com phenomenon, the growing threat of war in Iraq and putting a final emphatic full stop on all the joyous optimism of the past few years, 9/11, when the symbolic destruction of the World Trade Centre in New York ushered in a new, darker world order in which frivolity was seen as divisive and dangerous and effectively banished.

The effects of this cataclysmic trio of events were felt in every area of global life, but for industries built on the concepts of fun, hedonism and corporate largesse, it was particularly catastrophic. The dot-com crash, which began in March 2000, where young, inexperienced internet companies, which had been overvalued to the tune of billions by greedy investors eager to jump on the technology bandwagon, suddenly collapsed like a house of cards. This sent shares plummeting, and effectively pulled the rug out from the corporate hospitality world. There was a nervousness in big business that hadn't existed before. Budgets were reined in and social events curtailed. Then, over the next months a different kind of wariness crept into the collective consciousness as questions started to be asked about exactly what was going on in Saddam Hussein's Iraq, so crucial to the world's oil supply. These concerns would eventually result in the invasion of Iraq in March 2003. But more than anything else it was 9/11 that put paid to the notion of conspicuous displays of wealth, of which lavish parties are the most visible example. All of a sudden, the West was forced to confront how it was viewed by a large proportion of the world – immoral, unprincipled, interested only in money and personal gratification. America launched its 'War on Terror', portraying itself as the champion of free speech and democracy. People were scared to venture out of their houses, scared of crowds, scared to travel by plane. After the excesses of the late 1990s and the hangover of the millennium, the tragedy of 9/11 was the ultimate sobering up. It seemed like the party was well and truly over.

The reckoning, when it came, was harsh.

Enjoyment for enjoyment's sake was no longer cool. Hedonism and greed were partially what had got us into this mess, went the prevailing wisdom, and nobody wanted to be seen to be displaying or celebrating either. Bookings were way down, spirits flagged even further. The entire newly minted events industry swung in the balance as world markets waited with baited breath to assess the long-term fallout from the catastrophic events of 2001.

At Oaklands Road, Theme Traders regrouped and took stock. Though they lost half their bookings practically overnight, now more than ever they were grateful for their 'no job too small' policy and for having the prop hire business to fall back on. While the rest of the world seemed locked into a paralysis of limbo, David and Kim and their team quietly got on with the business of making and leasing out props and organising the more subdued, muted events that were still taking place.

The great thing about having stumbled accidentally into a business is that you're more stoical about the prospect of having to leave it. The Jamillys loved working in the events industry and were hoping against hope that it would recover, but they knew that if it didn't, they'd be able to take the skills they'd learned and the experience they'd accrued and set up in some other field. Not for nothing were they the grandchildren of the nomadic David Jamilly (the first).

Fortunately it never came to that. The markets gradually recovered, people started flying again, the banks realised their money was still safe (for now!) and that the global dip of the past two years had been just that – a dip. The events industry which had come so close to not making it past its infancy, slowly put its head once again above the parapet and started shuffling back to its feet. After the head-down approach of the previous months, suddenly a new note of defiance crept in. 9/11 had been an assault on our very way of life. Why should we bow to that? Having fun and the pursuit of happiness was one of the very cornerstones of Western philosophy – shouldn't we be defending that instead of apologising for it?

Back in Cricklewood, the phones, which had never gone completely silent, were once again ringing off the hook. The big finance companies, which had kept an uncharacteristically low profile over the preceding months, started strutting their stuff once more. There was still plenty of money around, house prices were still rocketing, bonuses were healthy, why shouldn't we celebrate the fact that we'd taken the worst the terrorists could throw at us, and we were still stronger than ever?

The parties began again, and new generations of undergraduates flocked to university to study event management. Why not? Everyone would always need social functions, wouldn't they? Hadn't we just proved that nothing would stop the West from partying?

Corporations were back in the business of hospitality, although the scale of the events was slightly different. The noughties had ushered in an era of environmental awareness and companies had to be careful about the size of their carbon footprints. Events became more localised as the global corporations stopped flying personnel from one world city to another, opting instead for multiple smaller events rather than one huge communal one.

For Theme Traders, the mid 2000s ushered in a period of sustained but steady expansion. The purchase of the farm in Leighton Buzzard was followed by the opening of an office in Edinburgh. Staff numbers grew from twenty to forty to sixty all working flat out as they struggled to cope with their burgeoning order book.

This was the era of Harry Potter mania, as party planners swooped on all things wizardly and magical. Fancy dress outfitters throughout the land ran out of pointy hats, broomsticks and cauldrons. The huge success of the Friends Reunited website invoked a rash of nostalgia-influenced events – any excuse to dress up in too-small school uniforms with ties around our heads was gratefully seized upon. Britney was huge, so was Eminem. Everything was about attitude.

As the decade progressed, parties became less about theme than about style. We had a new James Bond, the slightly dangerous, ultra-cool Daniel Craig. Sophistication with a gritty edge was the order of the day. Restaurants were all about ambient lighting, cubed seating and clean lines. Cool rather than kitsch was the buzzword. In the warmer months, the emergence of the festival scene launched a whole new era of fashion and party theming: floral wellies, fairy lights threaded through trees, long straight centre-parted hair with flower-garlanded cowboy hats.

As usual, Theme Traders was at the forefront of each changing trend, putting on some of the most seminal events of the time. In 2006, they were thrilled to be part of the Queen's 80th birthday party celebrations at Buckingham Palace. In addition to a fairy area and a pirate area, they paid tribute to the literary theme of the party by having a Beatrix Potter area complete with Mr McGregor's garden, all painstakingly recreated including potting shed and rows of vegetables. The vegetable plot was made by running pipes over the allotted area and then laying grass upside down over the top. Then, on the morning of the event, one of the staff was dispatched to New Covent Garden Market to select the freshest, most beautiful vegetables to 'plant' there. Afterwards, Kim sent Her Majesty a beautifully crafted photo album documenting the event, showing the Theme Traders' girls in the workshop painting the flowers and the toadstools like little elves. She received a letter, which she still treasures, thanking Theme Traders for all their work. While Kim always struggled with authority, it didn't stop her appreciating a strong female boss who knew exactly what she wanted and wasn't afraid to throw open the doors of her home to host a spectacular party. Hmmm… now why did that sound so familiar?

In tandem with the social whirl taking place globally, inside the Stadium at Oaklands Road, Theme Traders were becoming known for throwing their own anarchic brand of in-house party, usually instigated by Kim and often finishing up at her studio house in Hampstead Garden Suburb, where the long-suffering Michel grew used to coming home to find his living room sofa taken over by tutu-clad girls swigging champagne and exchanging raucous stories.

It might have sounded like a busman's holiday, but at Theme Traders, it was a case of any excuse for a staff party. And with so many props and costumes to hand, these were often wild and wonderful affairs, fuelled by a combustible mixture of heightened adrenalin levels caused by long hours working on a particular project, and a fair amount of alcohol. No wonder the company became legendary for inter-staff romances!

Caroline Tyrrell-Evans (project manager):

"One of my favourite parties was when each department had to choose a task from out of a hat, like my department had to do the Theme Traders rugby Haka. Richard's department had the Moulin Rouge and typically, it was any opportunity for cross-dressing. Out came the guys in corsets, fishnets and heels. Tom was the human windmill and was wrapped up in rope and plonked at the back of the stage, then Richard sat on the floor and the girls sat on top, with the guys being the legs and the girls the arms. I laughed so much I thought I was going to do myself an internal injury."

But despite all the hilarity, as the mid 2000s passed, there were the beginnings of unease. On the surface, there was no cause for alarm. The economy was booming, house prices were going through the roof. The UK was enjoying a period of sustained buoyancy and spending levels were higher than ever. iPods, laptops, digital cameras, modular sofas, Smart cars. Whatever was going, we wanted it. And yet if you listened carefully you could just make out the rumblings of concern. Where was all this money coming from? How long could it last? Were house prices over-inflated? Were mortgages too big? Who would pick up the shortfall if the housing market crashed?

The last of the big blow-out parties

The largest party TT has ever put together, both in terms of cost and logistics and the one that most stretched the company's resources to the limit, was to mark the bi-centenary of a national transport company in July 2007. The client had begun as a shipping company before branching into distribution, and boasted 5000 employees as well as offices and depots across the country. Initially the client had only a vague idea of what kind of party it wanted and it was left up to Natalie to go to the company's HQ for a brainstorming session with its PR people. The outcome was that they would spend £120 a head – no small amount when you consider the number of employees and they wanted a series of co-ordinated parties on the same date, rather than one enormous unworkable one. As it was such a huge sum, Natalie had to pitch for the contract against other event companies, suggesting three different locations for each party. Where TT had the edge was that it could provide a lot of what was needed from its own enormous stock and Natalie won the contract for the £500,000 party.

Celebrations were muted, however, as the full scale of the logistical nightmare of the occasion gradually became apparent. By the time the event was finished, Natalie had accumulated a dozen lever arch folders of information relating to it. The sticking point was the company's insistence that every last employee in the ten different locations across the country had to have exactly the same party as everybody else and each party had to begin and end at exactly the same time, feature exactly the same tables, chairs, decorations and chill out areas, complete with double beds for lounging around on. The TT props team were working around the clock for seven months leading up to the event. The operations team had an even more complicated job. Fifteen vans and six or seven articulated lorries had to be loaded and dispatched at the same time, to be sent to the different locations. Then the team had to divide up and unload each of them at the other end. The trucks went all over Britain – Solihull, Southampton, and at the end of the event they all had to be loaded back up again and the team had to race back to the Leighton Buzzard farm ready to unpack them all when the first one rolled in at 8am. It was a very long night (and morning after).

While the rest of the world carried on celebrating, at Theme Traders David and Kim were already starting to look ahead at what was coming. And it didn't look pretty.

The writing had started to appear on the wall in the mid 2000s when US interest rates suddenly shot up leaving home owners – many of whom had been lent money without much thought as to whether they'd be able to afford to repay it – struggling to pay their mortgages. The result was a domino effect of defaults and repossessions, leaving red-faced banks to foot the bill. Things got worse as the banks that had lent the money sold on their debts to other banks and by the summer of 2007, it was obvious that a huge financial crisis was looming.

At first it was just the banks who were running scared, but after a series of high profile financial institutions such as Bear

Stearns and Lehman Brothers collapsed, some taking investors' cash with them, everyone was panicking. House prices plunged, businesses closed and redundancies loomed.

The big financial corporations, which for some years had led the way in staging ever more impressive events, suddenly found themselves being forced to take a low profile as the blame for the economic crisis was heaped at their door. The high flyers who'd toasted their million pound bonuses with the finest champagne, listening to some of the world's biggest name entertainers at events organised by companies like Theme Traders, were suddenly persona non grata, their 'greed' widely blamed for causing what was becoming universally known as the Credit Crunch.

As videos of laid-off bank staff clearing their desks were broadcast around the world, and headlines were once again full of families trapped in negative equity or losing their homes, no financial institution could risk being seen to be spending money on anything that could be deemed frivolous.

Lavish events worth hundreds of thousands of pounds that had been booked for months or even years, were cancelled. Plans for a £150,000 Las Vegas themed event for an American Bank to be held at Old Billingsgate were dropped at the last minute. The bosses didn't feel they could justify the expense. Nearly one third of businesses admitted to having slashed their entertainment budgets, including the hallowed end of year party. Many of the larger events companies reported cuts in business of 50 per cent.

The downturn proved fatal for many of the smaller niche companies that had sprung up within the umbrella of the event management industry. The small businesses, which had been focusing just on just one element of the industry, whether table centres or flowers or balloons, and had been able to undercut the bigger companies by eliminating their large overheads, found themselves going under. They didn't have diversity to sustain the sudden drop in the numbers of available events.

With recession now an unavoidable reality, Theme Traders, like every other business, was forced to make some uncomfortable decisions.

Most devastating was the loss of personnel. From a height of sixty staff, the company cut down to forty. For a close-knit outfit with a culture of both working and playing hard together, to lose a third of its staff members was a major blow. But in the prevailing economic climate there was little option but to shave off expenditure wherever possible, batten down the hatches and try to struggle through.

Once again, Theme Traders' diversity proved its saving grace. The prop hire business was the nuts and bolts of the company. Even if people weren't throwing the big extravaganzas, there were still TV programmes like X Factor, EastEnders, Ant and Dec, Dr Who and Big Brother wanting custom-made furniture, or exhibition stands that required a giant rhinoceros or a fifteen foot Chinese Dragon.

For Kim and David, it was a nail-biting time. The duo who'd spent the best part of twenty years quite content to take a back seat and see where life took them, now found themselves with the fate of scores of people resting on their shoulders. Working so closely alongside their staff meant they knew exactly who had just taken on a bigger mortgage or was saving for a wedding or paying off a holiday. They knew exactly how important it was that the company stay operational and profitable.

Their oft-quoted mantra of 'never say no' came into its own. They'd always had a reputation for considering any job that came their way, no matter how small, and now they were glad of the steady stream of lower-budget jobs that came their way subsidising the downturn in the top-end events.

Heads down, Kim and David and the team hunkered down to weather the storm, which would end up capsizing so many of their contemporaries.

Mary Kay Eyerman (long-term client and organiser of the Datebook Ball):

"There have been times when economic conditions have made everyone pull together and think outside the box. David has been very adept at seeing change coming and he and Kim have demonstrated a unique ability to be flexible and stay ahead of the curve."

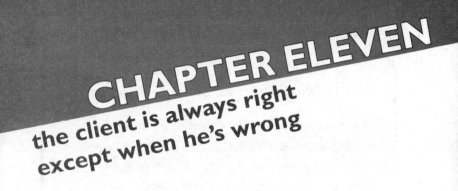

CHAPTER ELEVEN
the client is always right
except when he's wrong

As the years went on and Theme Traders gradually became experts in every field of event management and prop hire, they also, inadvertently, became highly skilled in a slightly more obscure area of expertise – the art of dealing with clients.

Handling clients who come to you asking for help in staging an event may not sound terribly challenging. You might assume it's a case of asking a) what's the budget? b) what's the occasion and c) what's the date, and off you go? Well, you might *think* that, but you'd be wrong.

Theme Traders has loyal clients who repeatedly come back and some of whom have become close friends. However, some clients are easier than others and David and Kim could now run their own degree course in recognising and handling all the distinct different types. Here's a potted digest:

The perfect client
The Holy Grail of all clients for any events organiser is one who comes with a blank chequebook and a completely open mind. Sadly, like Father Christmas, that client doesn't actually exist,

but there are plenty who are willing to take a step back and leave the creative ideas up to Kim and David and their staff, available to answer questions if necessary, but otherwise happy to let the experts get on with it.

David's favourite clients: the O'Farrells

"A sixty-something-year-old university professor and his wife, also an academic, the O'Farrells came to us a few years ago wanting us to plan a party for their golden wedding anniversary nearly two years hence. It wasn't a big budget event at all but they were a lovely couple and asked us to take charge of every single aspect of the party, from finding the venue, to organising the flowers. Every month or so, the couple would send a polite email checking on the progress of the event, but apart from that they stayed very much in the background. The result was that they received fantastic service because they were so delightful and everyone really wanted to make the party extra special for them. And it was. We found a country house with a barn and grounds and extra accommodation just outside Manchester, not far from where they lived, where they could go for the weekend and bring all their friends. And we organised the whole party – not too heavy production, but just meticulous attention to detail, and real care and commitment. They loved it, and so did we. It was one of those really special, fabulous events where you think 'ah, this is why I do this job'. Everybody who worked on that account was totally elevated by it."

The know-it-all

Unfortunately, not all clients are as happy to take a back seat. What Kim and David discovered as they negotiated their way through the ups of the 1990s and the rollercoaster of the early 2000s, was that just as everybody thinks they have a book in them, or knows more about interior design, or acting or comedy than those who do it for a living, so some clients coming to them for expert help secretly seemed to think that they could do it much better themselves, if only they had the time.

So rather than put themselves entirely in Theme Traders' capable hands, they come with their own ideas of how it should be done. Fair enough, after all it is their party. Except that sometimes the ideas don't quite marry with the budget, or with health and safety or with reality in general. Er, yes we could have a golden fountain in the middle of the room with gold-painted nymphs emerging on steel ropes, which wind up to the ceiling, and a 24-piece brass band, but is it really appropriate for an insurance company do? In the first floor boardroom? On a budget of X?

Where clients are keener on showing off their own creative imagination than encouraging or accepting the results of someone else's, even if that someone else does this for a living, there's bound to be a clash. Kim remembers last year's client who sent in a drawing of someone dressed up as a rotund giant snowman, which he wanted made up into costumes for a promotional event with a small ball for the head, and an enormous ball covering the body. "But if you have a perfectly spherical costume from the neck down to the feet, it'll be too wide for the person inside to get their arms through," Kim pointed out. "Not to mention actually getting through a doorway. Better to have a smaller sphere to the top of the legs with white tights and boots."

The client insisted, and drawings were exchanged back and forth until a compromise emerged – an anorexic looking snowman with a round section on top, segueing into a long thin section on the legs, not a patch on Kim's original design.

Cat Sterry's most stubborn client

"I'd been asked to make a wooden bar for a client out of very heavy mahogany sheets. They wanted the feel of a 1930s type of bar on a ship or something – very solid and art deco-style. I've made loads of bars over the years and there's a standard height that makes them look impressive but still reasonably easy to set up and transport and to make them functional as a prop. All the dimensions were agreed, but then the client announced they wanted castors on the bottom of the bar so that it could be easily moved around. I said 'well, okay, then I'll need to take a bit off the height because of the height of the castors'. 'No. We want it that height with the castors additional to that'. I knew it would be too tall. It would be overpowering, unwieldy and no one would be able to reach anything from the upper shelves, but the client refused to budge. 'I can make it any height you want, after all, you're the client,' I told them. 'But I make bars day in day out and I'm telling you, you'll think that's too high.' Nothing doing. Thankfully we got them to put it in writing because, of course, as soon as we got it on site, we have a call. 'Er, it's too high, can you get a crew down here to make it shorter or take the castors off.' Some people have to learn the hard way…"

"A lot of people are walking experts on everything and will go to the professionals in that field, wanting to prove to them just how much they know about their own subject," marvels David. "So they might come to me with a whacky idea, wanting me to say 'wow, that's amazing, you're so creative'. Well, that's fine, but in that case, what are you paying me for?"

The corporate power player

Despite being bohemians at heart, as the years passed Kim and David nevertheless grew very used to dealing with corporate clients and were as at home in a company boardroom surrounded by men in suits as back in Oaklands Road with their own t-shirted staff. Generally there was a healthy mutual respect between both parties, who acknowledged one another's differences, but also their strengths. However, one thing the Jamillys never grew used to was the power games that certain corporate clients insist on playing.

These could be anything from arbitrary changing of the brief or the budget, bullying tactics or trying to barter on an agreed price after the event.

In the heady days of the late 1990s, corporate clients could afford to flash their cash around, but as belts were tightened it became almost a point of honour among a certain type of client to try to shave money off their bills. It wasn't that unusual for a client to agree a price, pronounce themselves very satisfied with the event, and then demand a discount of ten per cent, intimating that such a drop would be seen favourably when it came to dishing out repeat business. "Great job, but our accounts department need to get an edge on this one, so we need a discount," is corporate speak for: drop the agreed fee or else. It might have been good business tactics in the corporate world, but for a conscientious company like Theme Traders, which prides itself on total transparency and fair profit-margin setting, losing ten per cent off a large budget event could worryingly destabilise the balancing of their books.

David's least favourite client: the power tripper

I was working on one very complicated and fantastically expensive, corporate party where the primary client was great. We had a very good relationship and they let me get on with my job. Then part-way through, when we'd already committed a lot of time and thousands of pounds to the project, a management consultancy, which was also involved in the event, came on board. I turned up for a meeting in a boardroom with everyone seated round this big round table and suddenly this woman started laying into me. 'Have you got details of this?' 'No, why not?' It was as if she was trying to prove to everyone else how hard-nosed she was – at my expense. I walked out of the meeting and rang Kim. 'I want to pull out,' I told her. 'I won't deal with someone like this.' Kim immediately backed me up, and I rang my original client. 'I've really enjoyed working with you, and I'd love to continue. I know this is going to be a fantastic event, but I can't work for more than one boss,' I told her. She took it all on board and went away. When she came back it was all sorted, everything would be channelled through her and I wouldn't have to deal with the other woman at all. In the end it was a fabulous event and we had a letter of thanks from the original client, and I never had to speak directly to the second woman again.

The window shopper

Meeting up with prospective clients and pitching ideas takes a huge amount of time and effort, and it can be deeply frustrating when it turns out a client isn't really serious about the event. David uses the analogy of a woman shopping for a special-occasion dress. She might already have seen just the dress she wants in a designer shop in Bond Street for £400, but before committing to paying for that, she wants to cast around to find out what else is out there. She might go into ten other shops and say 'show me all the types of dresses you have', but in the end all she's looking for is reassurance that the initial designer dress she secretly set her heart on is really the one she wants, and off she goes to get that one, happy that she's done all her research.

David and Kim know all too well that when a client comes into see them, after already forming an idea of exactly what they want, they could show them plans for the greatest party known to man, but they'd still get a 'thanks, but no thanks'. The problem is that, in the meantime, they've spent hours of valuable time basically reinforcing the client's existing ideal. So the client says 'give me a picture of the event'. You give them a picture of the event. Then the client says 'Hmmmm, can I see how it looks if you do X', so you do another picture incorporating X. The client is still unsure. 'Give me something to compare it to.' So that's another picture. The whole process can be endless, and yet each picture is an original creation. Theme Traders can come up with five or ten original creations for a client to turn round and say 'you know what, I think I'll go with the first guy.'

That's why they've learned wherever possible to ask for a token of commitment from the client. It might be that the client takes the time to actually come into the offices in Cricklewood, it might be a cash retainer, it might be that they agree to cover creative time if the project doesn't proceed.

> ### David's commitment maxim:
>
> "Any client who's not prepared to make some sort of commitment is in a one-way relationship and a one-way relationship means we can't wow the client, because they're not going to be communicating openly and honestly about what they want."

The same reservations hold true if Theme Traders gets invited to pitch for an event alongside others. Occasionally clients won't admit there are other companies involved who they're considering. That's an immediate no-no to Kim and David, who have built up a reputation for being direct and upfront. If there's no transparency, they won't be a part of it. Where clients are honest, they will sometimes agree to pitch, but there always has to be a realistic appraisal of how long they're willing to invest in the pitch. If a pitch takes a week to put together, that's a big chunk of time (and therefore money) for a busy company, so they have to weigh up carefully whether it's a worthwhile investment.

The demanding client

Some clients might agree a brief and then announce "I'm off to Dubai for six weeks and won't be back until the day of the party. Do what you can and I'll see you at the event." More typically though, a client will be over-involved rather than under. Wedding clients and Bar Mitzvah clients are the most demanding. Often they'll call every day for months leading up to the event and each call is a matter of life or death. "I'm not sure anymore whether I want the magenta or the antique pink. Please send a swatch around right away."

TV clients:

Theme Traders has established links with several long-running TV shows which make use of its props, quirky premises or expertise. One of the team's favourite clients is hit show The Apprentice, which regularly enlists the company's help in tasks that involve organising events, prop making or interior design. Particularly popular are the fundraising celebrity versions of the show in which household names compete to win tasks with the expert help of Theme Traders stalwarts to raise money for charity's such as Sport Relief. "Working with Gok Wan was one of the funniest experiences," says TT's Becky Handley. "They were supposed to be dressing a venue on a shoestring and he wafted in with all these big ideas of draping the place in amazing fabrics. I kept reminding him he was supposed to be on a budget and he'd seem to be taking it in, then he'd come out with some ridiculously outlandish, extravagant idea. He was great fun – although if he'd been a real client it might have been a bit of a problem!"

When time is money, a daily call debating whether the edging on the tablecloths should be plain or slightly waffled can make all the difference between coming in on budget, and someone being out of pocket. It doesn't help that Theme Traders has also evolved a very comprehensive (for comprehensive read 'complicated') operational system whereby every single call is logged and noted, with back up copies made, so that there's no chance of error. With so many different arms of the company, the potential for information being lost or not passed on is huge, which is why they're so strict about keeping records of everything. For the client, the fact they've changed from magenta to antique pink is crucial and for that decision not to be passed on could make all the difference between being satisfied or not, and it's a risk Kim and David are not prepared to take. The result is that Theme Traders generates a lot of paperwork. An *awful* lot of paperwork!

The other type of demanding client is the one who sets ridiculous time limits. A really short lead time means something will suffer – usually creativity. But equally a really long lead time, where clients call all the time for an event that's still six months off, can also cause problems. When a company has been at the top of their field for years, they instinctively know when something needs to be done and how long it will take, and they don't need the pressure that an over-anxious client can apply.

The combative client

Most clients take on an event manager so that they can either hand over responsibility for an occasion, or at least have someone to share the load. But occasionally people will see the company they've hired less as an ally than a whipping post for when things go wrong or even as a threat.

Even the clients with loads of money can be suspicious of how a company is spending it, or whether they're getting the best value, and it can be wearing having every single action queried, every penny accountable.

Becky Handley (project manager):

"When I first landed the job of organising a £100,000 party for an American oil billionaire, to celebrate his daughter's 21st birthday party, I was ecstatic. He wanted a Fairy Tales theme – exactly up my street. We had knights on real horses, an enchanted forest, swan contortionists and stilt-walkers dressed as trees. But it almost turned into a nightmare. He was constantly on the phone questioning whether I knew what I was doing as I was practically the same age as his daughter, and trying to beat the money down. I soon realised that just because someone is hugely rich, they still want to feel they're getting value for money and I had to really work hard to convince him that I did have the experience and I did know what I was talking about. We had a fiery relationship and even after I'd gained his trust, he was always blowing up at me, seeing how far he could push me, but I always managed to stay calm and in the end he stopped being quite so antagonistic and the party went off really well. As an event organiser, you have to be able to stand your ground in a very calm way. But it's not always easy."

Even when Theme Traders are sub-contracted by another event organiser, thereby eliminating direct contact with the client, there can be problems. Not surprisingly, fellow event organisers can make the most exacting of clients.

When Becky was working on transforming a room at a banqueting house along an Oriental theme for a highly-strung, freelance event organiser, she received a call at the office. The voice was so apoplectic with rage that it took a while for Becky to work out that the organiser was protesting about the size of the Chinese lanterns Becky's crew were currently rigging up. "They're too small! They're all wrong! You've ruined my career! I'm going to go bankrupt because of you!" As Becky sat open-mouthed listening to this tirade in the open plan offices, David started passing her a succession of notes. "You don't have to listen to this". "Hang up". But Becky heard the woman out until she eventually (very eventually) ran out of steam and then Becky told her, very politely, she'd send someone to Chinatown to get some new lanterns. By the time she arrived on site later that day, the new larger lanterns were all strung up and looking wonderful and the previously vitriolic event organiser presented her with a bottle of champagne by way of apology. But Becky had learned two valuable lessons: 1) Don't take it personally – sometimes the client just needs to vent; 2) David and Kim will *always* support their staff.

The everything-over-the-top client

David and Kim would always rather a client has too much imagination rather than not enough, but sometimes it can be hard to get a client to accept that having 150 semi-naked models descending from helicopters in the middle of Piccadilly Circus, accompanied by an orchestra of body-painted harpists each suspended from their own individual, lorry-mounted crane isn't the most straightforward or feasible of ideas.

Though they'll never say 'no' if something is achievable within the client's budget, occasionally the laws of physics (or more usually of health and safety) cause them to try to steer the event in a slightly different direction. But there are some clients who will not be deterred from their grand vision. One of these was Lord P whose event will forever be remembered as The Live Elephant (that wasn't) Party.

Lord P and the live elephant (that wasn't) party:

One morning, Theme Traders received a very peculiar email. "I want a party. I own a castle, and I want a live elephant." It was signed simply 'Simon'. Natalie emailed Simon back and asked him to call her with a few more details. Two days later, her desk phone rang. The caller was Simon P, a British eccentric living in tax exile in the Caribbean, but wanting a party five weeks hence at his own private castle in Ireland to celebrate three milestone family birthdays, his own, his son Tom's and that of his father, Lord P. He announced that he was flying to Ireland the following week and to save time, Natalie agreed to meet with the three prospective party hosts at the family castle. Of the three, only Tom had any idea what he wanted from the party — a live elephant, wandering freely around. Apart from that, they had no clue about food, marquees, anything. Moreover, Simon had no concept of budget and Natalie found herself in the slightly unusual position of having to rein in some of his more extravagant suggestions. The money for the party had to come from the P family trust, who therefore all had to be invited to the party, just to make sure they approved the funds. In the end the budget was £250,000.

It took ten days to build the party sets. There was a huge marquee outside and several tents specifically designated as casino areas, as well as a few empty rooms in the castle itself. Initially the guest list had been agreed at 500, representing a veritable who's who of Britain's rich and famous, but Simon kept inviting more and more people, to the consternation of the caterers. Proper casino tables were brought in from Monte Carlo. Natalie assumed it would be play-betting as, of course, there was no gambling licence. Just as well she didn't discover until afterwards that it was all very serious – so serious, in fact, that the minimum table stake was £2000.

Full-on security was required to police the party as when word got out about just who was expected to turn up, Fleet Street became desperate to gatecrash. A heli-pad had to be constructed because so many of the guests wanted to arrive by helicopter. The party started at 8pm on the Saturday evening and was still going strong on Sunday night as the richest of the rich let their hair down and, as Natalie later said "behaved badly in just about any way you can imagine."

When it was written up in the gossip columns, it was described as the best party of the season, but there was one notable absence – the live elephant, the only thing that had been expressly requested, proved sadly impossible. Not altogether unsurprisingly, when faced with the prospect of hundreds of worse for wear aristocrats and celebrities, rubbing shoulders with a free-ranging, six-ton elephant, insurance companies hadn't exactly leapt over themselves to offer cover. In fact, the 'Elephant Element' had proved something of a party deal breaker.

The 'too many chefs' client

With corporate clients, instructions often come not from an individual but a committee whose job it is to manage hospitality for that company. This can be a big plus when it comes to diffusing potential personality clashes between client and party planner, but can also cause communication problems, particularly when there are complicated power dynamics within the committee.

Kim will never forget the corporate client who asked Theme Traders to organise a big sit-down function at a hotel. Most of the committee were agreed that they wanted a high tea, but there was one individual who felt strongly that the occasion should be a lunch-time affair. Unfortunately, he was the one in charge of printing up and sending out invitations. At 12.30 on the day of the function, the Theme Traders team was already in place making sure they had plenty of time to arrange food, table centres and décor in time for the 3.30 kick-off. They were surprised, but not unduly alarmed, when a guest wandered in as they were setting up – it often happened that the odd guest would get the wrong end of the stick and turn up horribly early. But when more and more guests flooded in behind him, the rather unwelcome truth began to dawn. They had all come expecting a lunch function. Starting NOW. Hurriedly, staff downed their staple guns and helium cylinders, donned aprons and assumed their positions, while in the kitchen frantic efforts were made to convert what was to have been a sumptuous tea, into a make-shift lunch. Fortunately, they pulled it off – but only just.

David's mantra for the best possible client relationship:

"Imagine there are 63 different elements involved in an event. If you had an infinite budget you could work with every single element and style, twist and theme them to make it exceptional. Of course, most clients don't have that sort of budget. But if we really understand the client, if they're working with us and there's two way communication and respect, if we've got time and we're not being rushed or harassed, we can probably twist up five or six of those elements and still make it a big 'wow' that will bowl the client over, at a more economical level."

The over-friendly client

Kim and David value their clients greatly and many go on to become firm friends. However, while an event is being planned, with client and project manager often spending long hours together organising the finer details, it is possible for the lines between professional and personal to become a little blurred. Becky once organised a very elaborate Bar Mitzvah for a client who was so wrapped up in the preparations for the party that for two years Becky became practically the most important person in her life. Even after the party was over, the client couldn't quite let go and would ring Becky for a chat and tell her how much she missed her.

Kim remembers a client falling for one of her performers, Maz (she of the palmistry fame) who helped out at a high profile event. The morning after the event the client's wife phoned the Theme Traders office in a rage. "A member of your staff has stolen a bottle of wine and a hat," she fumed. Pointless to tell her that her husband had given Maz the gifts as part of his (failed) seduction attempt.

These days, Kim and David are careful to prime their workers that when it comes to on-the-job client relationships, it pays to be friendly – but not too friendly.

CHAPTER TWELVE
the psychology of parties

Human beings have always enjoyed a good 'do'. From the earliest written histories, there are records of feasts and communal gatherings to mark or celebrate special occasions or events. We humans have a basic need to interact with others, to observe rituals or rites of passage, to show off to our friends and neighbours, to make offerings to the gods or generally cheer ourselves up.

But parties didn't become big business until after the post-war period and it was 1986 when the first book that bore any resemblance to event management appeared. It was by Lady Elizabeth Anson, cousin to the Queen, who had been running her own upper-class party planning business since the 1960s. Called *Lady Elizabeth Anson's Party Planner's Book*, it was full of interesting suggestions on how to play party games like sardines (during which guests would emerge from cupboards either "crushed or flushed").

After that, party organising took on a life of its own, but interestingly the motivation behind giving parties has remained essentially the same, and the key to successful event management still lies in understanding exactly what it is the client is hoping to get from the party. In detective stories, it's often the case that once you understand the murderer's motivation, you're half way towards cracking the case. The same holds true with party planning (well, apart from the murderer bit obviously).

The first thing Kim and David and the rest of the project managers do, when they're considering a new brief, is to try to work out why the client wants to hold the party.

> **David:**
>
> "You need to be able to hear what someone means, no matter what words they're actually saying,"

Some common reasons for throwing a party:

1. Showing off

Let's be honest, we all do it. Built a new kitchen extension? Invite your mates round for dinner to show it off. Been promoted? Throw a party to show all the doubters just how well you've done. In the corporate world, the showing off reached its peak around the time of the millennium, with each company trying to outdo its rivals to prove just how successful/generous/ forward thinking it was.

These days, the motivation is less likely to be about boasting and more about subtly getting it right. Where clients are going for the big-budget, high-end events, they often want to show that they've reached a certain level of effortless sophistication and luxury. In order to help them achieve that, David and Kim and the staff have to understand that world – which might sound like an excuse for staying in some of the world's most opulent hotels and eating out at the finest restaurants all in the name of 'research', but that's their story and they're sticking to it!

> ### David's explanation for why his stay in the 7* hotel Burj-Al-Arab Hotel in Dubai made complete business sense:
>
> "Private people want an individualised, bespoke, luxury service and they want all the attention that you'd get in the 7* hotel in Dubai. I've stayed there, because if you don't understand it, how can you know what it is people expect? If you haven't stayed somewhere like that, where the lobby is made with gold leaf, marble, granite and crystals, how can you comprehend that a room can cost a million pounds – just to build that one room, or that they can charge thousands of pounds a night or whatever they charge. If you get that perspective in your head then you understand the level of luxury some people expect, and if you're dealing in that market you have to understand those expectations. If you don't, you don't have a chance."

2. Keeping up with (or better still, going one better than) the Jones'

Sometimes it's not the desire to be seen to have achieved a certain level that drives clients, but the need to match, or even better ones peers or rivals. We've already seen how the big financial players vied to outdo each other during the boom party period of the late nineties and turn of the century, flying in bigger name stars to entertain the guests, serving better champagne, giving out more extravagant goodie bags. On a smaller scale some of the private clients, particularly those who'd hired Theme Traders to organise a Bar Mitzvah or a wedding might also be driven by a need to make sure their event outshines the one their friend or neighbour or cousin had had the week or month before. Knowing that the client's motivation is to compare favourably with the nearest competition rather than to be the most innovative or relaxed or adventurous saves a lot of time (and aggravation) in the long run.

3. Having themselves a wonderful time

If a client is shelling out a lot of money for a party, it sounds like a no-brainer that they'd want to enjoy it. And yet many party-givers don't expect to have a great time themselves, assuming that they'll be too busy making sure other people relax and have a memorable occasion. A free pass to enjoy your own party is perfectly achievable, but it will usually cost you. If your motivation is to sit back and be a king or queen for a night, that's going to be more expensive because every single aspect of the running of the party will have to be taken over by someone else.

4. Making a statement

People throw parties as a way of sending out clear messages to others. Some are very obvious – we're serious about each other, we've had a successful year, we are so happy to have moved. Others are less overt – we're still very much a couple, we're not going down the tubes, we're doing very well thank you very much.

The psychology of corporate clients

Understanding how the motivation of corporate clients differs from that of private ones is essential. With corporate clients,

A private affair

One of the weirdest motivations was the client who wanted to make up to his wife for some obviously quite monumental transgression. Approaching Theme Traders with a budget of £30,000, he wanted to hire a restaurant for his own private use, which would be filled on every surface with white roses, his wife's favourite flower, and beautifully decorated in the most romantic style. Theme Traders was also to supply a pianist to sit in the corner, unobtrusively tinkling gently lilting melodies in the background while the couple enjoyed some intimate time together over a menu of the finest aphrodisiac food known to man... Except it didn't quite turn out like that.....Whatever the client was making amends for, it had to be pretty major. The wife was in no mood for flowers, or music, or romance. From the minute they sat down, the couple argued, and the louder the pianist played, the louder the arguments. Every time he stopped they'd glare over at him, whichever insult they were about to hurl quivering on the tips of their tongues, so he had no option but to go back to playing, this time even louder, to cover up the increasingly venomous exchanges. The poor pianist's fingers were stinging from playing, his back ached from sitting and his bladder was about to burst, but he dare not step away from the piano for fear of what he might have to listen to if he stopped playing.

the aim is not only for the guests to have a good time, but also to come away with a better understanding of what the company or a particular department within it, is about, or to win greater company loyalty.

So the structure of event will be different. There'll be protocol, maybe a speech, or a few speeches. It's vital to assess with the client beforehand exactly how much speech-making there's going to be, so that the flow or sequence of the event can be adjusted accordingly, incorporating all those necessary elements without it seeming stilted.

But the psychology of parties isn't only about client expectations; it's also about knowing how to take the strain of holding a party off the client's shoulders. So it's about knowing when a client wants to be kept in the loop on all developments so that he feels like he's still in control; or, when he wants to sit back and relinquish the reins, not being bothered by the inevitable things that go wrong in the execution of an event requiring an urgent reverting to Plan B.

Hannah Smith (head of wardrobe):

"It was 4am and we were laying down carpet on a yacht in docklands ahead of an upmarket event the next morning. We were working against the clock, but nobody warned us the room was uneven. Every time someone walked on the matting we'd put down, it bubbled up. We were faced with two dire choices – leave a panicked message for the client, or call David. No prizes for guessing we called David who immediately dispatched a team down to the docks armed with big needles to sew the carpet together by hand so it couldn't curl or gather. The client got an uninterrupted night, and we were left with bags under our eyes and lots of needle punctures in our thumbs. But in the end, everyone knew their role."

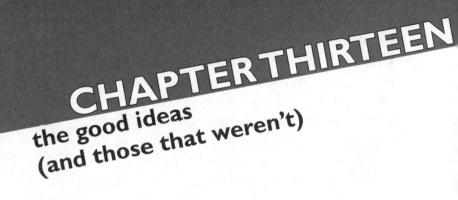

CHAPTER THIRTEEN
the good ideas
(and those that weren't)

As the recession loomed, Theme Traders decided it was time to diversify yet again; after all it was the company's ability to function under many different umbrella descriptions – prop hire, costume makers, set designers, location finders – that had stood it in such good stead up until this point.

Kim threw herself into developing the company website. Typically, despite leaving school with no formal qualifications, her response to the daunting challenge of keeping up with modern technology wasn't "that's too scary I'll get a man who does," but "how hard can it be?" Particularly when she discovered that getting a man who does would cost upwards of £500 a day.

But it wasn't plain sailing. At the end of the 1990s Kim had been outraged to discover that one of their competitors had brought up the domain name themetraders.net. Even though she complained to the regulating body and the name was eventually returned, it left a sour taste in her mouth and Theme Traders had immediately bought up every variation on their name. But it wasn't until years later that she really got to grips with just how powerful a tool the Web could be. She and Cat set about familiarising themselves with IT and website design and painstakingly photographing and cataloguing every single prop in the company's vast warehouses. They also suggested various party themes, showcased previous parties they had organised, and laid out the different services the company provided from flowers to room styling and product launches.

The website proved a fantastic business tool, enabling prospective clients to see at a glance the breadth and scope that Theme Traders had to offer.

Other ideas haven't been so well received. The notion of themed weddings was bandied about at one point. Wow Weddings was to be an offshoot of the main company and catering for, well, couples who wanted to tie the knot dressed in Medieval costumes or as characters from *Gone with the Wind* or who wanted a fairytale wedding themed entirely in purple. After a less than lukewarm response, it was quietly dropped, as was the other brain wave – themed funerals. Not only could this have been construed as slightly disrespectful to the dead, it was also a logistical nightmare.

The theory was that people would arrange their own themed funeral in advance, choosing a bespoke service that reflected their own interests and personalities and freeing up their loved ones from the agonising burden of having to organise an event that fully did justice to the dearly departed.

For a few heady weeks, the idea gained popularity around Oaklands Road, with people throwing themselves into the possibilities offered by a themed funeral company. But gradually reality started to dawn. It was fine if clients died in a nice orderly, evenly-spaced fashion, say one a week, but what would happen if they all popped their clogs on the same day? Or on Christmas Day? And, with each event needing to be meticulously prepared, how on earth would they get enough advance warning that their services were to be required? Eventually, with some reluctance, the themed funerals idea died a death. In a manner of speaking.

Becky's good idea:

"On New Year's Eve, 2007, I was asked to present live, hourly updates on BBC Breakfast News, advising viewers on how to throw the ultimate New Year's Eve party. I was filmed in one of the Theme Traders meeting rooms, adorned with balloons, party hats and of course, champagne. Even though the first bulletin aired at 5am, I decided it would be a great idea to start drinking the champagne to calm my nerves. Oh dear. By the time the second segment went out at 6, I was considerably more relaxed. By 7am, I was on a roll. 8am found me wearing a little party hat tied around my chin with elastic and spouting on as if I was Fern Britton. As I stumbled upstairs at 9 to begin my day in the office (and don't forget 31 December is one of our busiest days), I was three sheets to the wind. David called to congratulate me on my performance. My struggle to align the phone with my ear, must have given the game away. 'You're drunk,' he said incredulously. With my party hat still perched askew on my head, and a glass of champagne in one hand, it was hard to deny it. 'For goodness sake go home and sleep it off,' he told me, which I very gratefully did. Apparently you couldn't tell what was going on in the broadcasts – I just seemed to be growing increasingly animated. Still, I don't think I'll be searching for the clips on YouTube any time soon."

CHAPTER FOURTEEN
being the boss

> **Stanley Bloom (Theme Traders accountant):**
>
> "Conflict between the two bosses at Theme Traders can be daunting to witness but it often leads to brilliant spontaneous ideas."

When they (rather reluctantly) shouldered the mantle of management, the last thing Kim and David intended was to fall into a good cop-bad cop style of bossness. Occasionally, however, their contrasting personalities have made that comparison inevitable. The truth is it's their differences that make for the creative spark, which fires the whole company. While they were growing up, the Jamilly siblings bickered constantly, but rarely had major fallings out. It's always been hard to rile the legendarily unflappable David, while Kim, who can erupt like Mount Vesuvius, won't allow a quarrel to fester.

Juliana Muir (project manager) on Kim:

"Once, in the early days, when I'd just started working for Theme Traders, I tried to offer an opinion on something and got a real earful from Kim. I was mortified, but once I got to know her better, I realised that Kim just says whatever comes into her head at the time. If she doesn't like something she'll say it's rubbish but you shouldn't take it personally. She'll come out with something really blunt, but ten minutes later you'll be chatting away as if nothing has happened. It's forgotten about and dealt with. Move on."

Those childhood patterns continued into adulthood. At work, David was always the laid back one, who listened quietly and gave considered advice. Kim steamed in, saying exactly what she thought – even when what she thought wasn't terribly diplomatic (although usually – and irritatingly – right). Over the years, while the business grew around them, their individual styles of management remained, by and large, the same and astonishingly, they *still* have very few big fallings out.

That doesn't mean to say they're always in perfect harmony though. Come off it – they *are* siblings after all! Kim, who incidentally prefers a patriarchal/matriarchal comparison to good cop/bad cop says they try not to argue in front of 'the children' (i.e. the staff), but that a certain amount of argument is inevitable, and even healthy.

When the two quarrel in board meetings, it can be a tricky call for staff. If they back Kim, David is apt to insist they're just

buttering her up to get into her good books. If they back David…
there are two possible reactions – either they'll find themselves
on the receiving end of one of Kim's legendary bollockings, or
she'll sit back and say 'okay I'm wrong'. It's hard to say which
response is more disarming.

But woe betide the staff member who tries to play one sibling
off against the other, as one ex-staff member (very ex) once tried
to. Every family is the same – you're allowed to gripe about each
other to your hearts' contents, but if an outsider tries to join in, you
immediately close ranks. *Especially* if you all work together.

Peter Selby (director of the Westminster Boating Base venue and long-term friend):

"Kim can sell coal to Newcastle. She's incredible. I've
never seen anything like it in my life. But if you need
something done on the business end you ask David."

Kim:

"I'm very happy working with David. I never get tired
of arguing with him. The problem is, sometimes he gets
upset and won't talk to me. I know the arguments don't
matter. If there's something to be done, I know he can
make it happen and he knows I can make it happen. We
might not do it in the same way, but we'll get the same
end result. By having our fights, we bash it out."

Anyone who remembers those arguments over whose turn it is in the bathroom or whose turn it *isn't* to do the washing up/walk the dog/give up their bed so that grandma can sleep over will take their hats off to the Jamillys for having clocked up nearly forty years working shoulder to shoulder, but there have been times when it has all got too much, even for them.

A few years back, Kim had enough. She was feeling burned out at work, bored at home and generally in need of a change. Every day she trailed into the office in Cricklewood without her usual bounce and energy, and every evening she returned home to Hampstead Garden Suburb out of sorts.

"I need a sabbatical," she announced to Michel.

"Hmph," came the non-committal response.

"I need a sabbatical," she told David. This time the reply was more emphatic.

"No."

This was followed by the typical sibling response: "*I'd* like to take a sabbatical but I've got a company to run. If I can't take one you can't either. *It's not FAIR!*"

But Kim was adamant. She had to get away. She'd go off for six months or a year, recharge her batteries and then return home with renewed vigour. Either that or go to Brazil, get a new identity and never be seen again.

She set about arranging her grown up gap trip. Always having loved skiing and mountain scenery, what could be more appropriate than spending some time in the Alps? On impulse she decided to hire a chalet for the entire winter season. The decision felt so liberating, she just couldn't understand why she hadn't done it sooner. Anyone would be suffering from burn-out after working so hard for so long. She deserved some me-time.

At the office, David kept up an injured air, pointedly not asking her how her arrangements were getting on, or whether she'd remembered to take out travel insurance or brush up on her French. It was much the same story at home with Michel, but Kim ignored any hostile vibes. Once she decided on something, she followed it through, and she was not about to be dissuaded from the adventure of a lifetime.

As her departure date approached, she could hardly hide her excitement. Going round the office on her last day to say goodbye to the staff was emotionally fraught, but she knew she was doing the right thing and inside was secretly exploding with anticipation. Inevitably, there were a lot of tears and a lot of hugs. Privately some wondered if she'd ever return.

By the time the big day dawned, Kim was itching to be off. She'd never done the whole travel the world bit, having gone straight in to work for Victor at Laurence Corner. It was like a delayed adolescence (except with more money) and she couldn't wait to get started. Waving a jaunty goodbye to Michel, she drove off to get the ferry to France, feeling smug at having remembered to insure her car for a year's driving abroad, even if it had set her back £2000. In typical Kim style, she hadn't bothered to change any currency before setting off, but she had a walletful of credit cards to see her through.

Once safely on French soil, she realised her petrol gauge was on empty and happily pulled into a petrol station to fill up. One problem. It was Sunday so only the automated pay-at-pump pumps were working. And they didn't accept her UK cards.

Kim took a long look at her petrol gauge, and then at the pump with its long line of 0s. And then she did what any grown-up, adventure-seeking independent woman setting off on a solo sabbatical would do. She called her husband.

Having to ring Michel for help just hours after leaving was but a temporary setback. Once the problem with the petrol had been sorted and Kim was back behind the steering wheel with a full tank, her giddy lightheadedness returned. This was the life – speeding down the largely empty auto-route with music blaring out and not a care in the world.

Arriving at the ski resort only reinforced her conviction that she'd made a most excellent decision. The skiing was great, there were loads of people to talk to and best of all, she didn't have to think about work. The first couple of days flew by in a whoosh of black runs, ski lifts and après-ski toddies. But towards the middle of that first week, she started to feel a little, well, lonely. It was all very well being surrounded by all this stunning fresh Alpine scenery, but she was starting to get just a teensy bit curious about what was going on back in grimy, congested Cricklewood. And though it was great meeting lots of new people, she missed being around familiar faces. She called Michel.

"Oh, it's fabulous here. Absolutely wonderful. I'm loving every minute of it. Do you fancy coming for a holiday?"

On the Thursday evening, just four days after waving his wife off for her huge adventure, Michel flew out to join her. And when it came time for him to return home on the following week, Kim packed up all her stuff and came home with him. Her much vaunted gap year had lasted just eleven days.

It wasn't just the indignity of having to slope back into the office barely a week after making such a dramatic exit that Kim had to endure on her return. She also discovered that David, feeling sorry for Michel being abandoned in such a cavalier way, had arranged a boys' trip to Latvia the coming weekend complete with a visit to a marriage bureau, where Michel would be sorted out with a new wife. One who wouldn't go gallivanting round the

What Kim's sabbatical-that-wasn't proved:

"It illustrates Kim's bullishness," says David. "If someone says to Kim 'you can't do that', she will stop everything else and find a way to do it. It's something very deep. I'm exactly the same. I'll say 'sod you' and I'll shelve everything to do it. Then you've got two people saying 'we can do it' it's quite a strong force. It's not a gamble. We do know what we're doing. We have a track record of making things happen."

world, but would be quite happy to stay home. To her outrage, the trip went ahead despite her premature return home, with Michel, David and the friend they'd gone with all enjoying a lovely dinner out with their prospective new brides. Meanwhile, Kim sat home alone, trying not to remember that she ought, by rights, to be whizzing down a ski slope at 20mph.

Still, the one good thing about Kim's Sabbatical-That-Wasn't was that it cured her of both her wanderlust and her worries that she should be doing something else with her life. Nowadays when she counsels her younger staff members, she always tells them never to worry about changing their minds. If you feel something's not right, she urges them, pull out – even if it was your idea in the first place. It's your mind, you have the right to change it.

It's not only Kim and David's differences that have made for such a strong working partnership. Despite their wildly opposing managerial sides, they're bonded by fundamentals, like shared values and a common motivating force, which is less about making a profit and more about proving they can do it – whatever 'it' might be.

David explains what drives the Jamillys:

"We have always been motivated by fighting the odds. The money itself has never been the issue. It's been balancing the money-making side against the odds of succeeding. Sometimes the money side becomes too important and that's tedious. If you could do it without the money being involved – just doing bigger and better parties, it'd be great. We didn't set out to make a fortune, we set out to make a living. In those days, the motivation was to prove to our dad we could do well and part of that is having the tokens people use to judge if you're doing well, which are to do with money. But that was never a motivation. Kim wouldn't have a clue how much money she's got in the bank, or indeed if she's got any money in the bank. I have to be aware of those things because we've got cash commitments to people. If we had no commitments, we'd have no staff. I probably wouldn't be interested in having a bank account either way. Success to us is about achievement and fighting the odds, running against the tide, being maverick. Those things are exciting."

They also share some valuable characteristics – like the ability to make an instant decision and not agonise about it afterwards.

When Turpins Yard, the premises down the street from the original 'Stadium' came up for sale, David instinctively knew he wanted to buy it. Even though at the time (2002) the £1.25m price tag seemed extortionate, he knew it was a good investment. Besides, it being a borrowing-a-cup-of-sugar distance from the existing Theme Traders set-up made it too tempting to turn down. Sold, to the man in the TT t-shirt! Similarly when Maurice the Butcher mentioned there was a 100 acre farm up for sale in Leighton Buzzard that would make the ideal base for storing bulkier and less used props, the Jamillys insisted on seeing the place that very same day. Maurice rang the owner and fixed an appointment two hours later and Kim and David had committed to buying the farm by the end of that first afternoon. Ditto the decision to buy the other string of warehouses and some properties in Scotland.

Of course, not every decision they make is the right one (remember the sabbatical-that-wasn't?) but nine out of ten work out well, and in the one case in ten that doesn't, well you can always make another decision.

Elissa Capizzi-Taylor (project manager):

"Working with Kim and David is good because you always know where you stand with them. Everything is in the open and they are always around so you can talk to them as and when problems come up, and they try to teach all the staff about how the whole business operates, so you don't feel you're just isolated doing your little bit."

Mary Kay Eyerman (client):

"David and Kim are the kind of people one never forgets. They do not suffer fools lightly but are very restrained – well at least David is – in commenting on people or events. Kim is outspoken, but has a big heart and a love of life, which is simply fantastic. My dear Godmother used to say that there are people in life with whom you are 'simpatico'. That perfectly describes our relationship with David and Kim."

Clifford Gee (friend):

"Together, Kim and David create a fantastic balance. David is very focused on the business side with clear directions about where the company is heading, and Kim is always coming up with different creative ideas."

Jane Wormleighton (Kim's childhood friend):

"Kim at 11 and Kim today haven't changed a great deal. Kim was a girl in between two brothers, so she was very strong-willed, determined, outgoing, confident and could talk to anyone in any given situation. Kim is ballsy. That's the word. She speaks her mind, always has done. The balance between her and David is fascinating because where she will be outspoken, David can take a perspective in a slightly more controlled way. It's a perfect combination."

CHAPTER FIFTEEN
throwing a party – david's step-by-step guide

If David and Kim had a pound for every time they get asked the secret of a truly memorable party, they'd have… well, a LOT of money. Of course, every party is different – every host has different expectations and every guest different criteria. But you can't stage 2000 events a year for twenty years without learning a thing or two about what makes a party go with a bang, and the Jamillys have pretty clear ideas of how it is (and isn't) done.

Structure

There's a widely held myth that the best parties are spontaneous, unorchestrated events, where all the elements magically work together without any effort or design. Occasionally, as with the parties at Theme Traders that start with a crate of champagne in the office at the end of a busy week and end in a full-blown rave at Kim's house wearing wigs and fancy dress, completely impromptu events can work precisely because of their spontanaiety. But with a planned event, it has to be structured to within an inch of its life. David sometimes even plots out the sequence of an event on music paper like a musical score, so he can more easily see and plot the pattern and flow.

"Sometimes spontaneous things happen in life that are enjoyable," he acknowledges, "but that's not in the context of what I call an event or what the events industry should call an event, or what one would call a party. Getting a collection of people in a room together doesn't automatically make it a party, in the same way that bumping into a couple of friends in the street and going for a coffee isn't a party. It can be fun, but it's not an event."

Events are structured in terms of sequence and mood and a successful party organiser will plan both meticulously.

Budget

David: "There's no set amount of money that guarantees you a good party. The essence of a good party is to understand your guests, to understand their origins and expectations, and to understand your own motivation in having the event."

Working out a budget is key to throwing a good party. Once you know what parameters you're working to, it's much easier to fill in the blanks. Stick to what you can afford. If you go over, you're not going to feel relaxed about the party and you'll probably end up cutting corners later on. Work out what elements are most crucial to you and remember guests won't remember that the food was so-so or the wine was cheap if they've been 'wowed' by the theme, or the effects or the overall styling. Understand yourself and your guests, work out what will make them feel excited and special, and use inexpensive tricks, because after all, it's the theatre of an event which will stay in people's minds.

Theatre

The cheapest way to inject theatre into your event is to involve one of our less used senses, like touch. The second you bring touch into an event, it's likely to make it much more memorable for your guests. So being taken by the arm into an event, is immediately an incredibly inexpensive way to make an impact. If the fabric you have on the table is a fabric you don't expect to see – sacking for example, or plain brown wrapping paper (going for more expensive, it could be silk) it throws people straight away. That's the magic of touch.

There's an incredibly successful restaurant in London, which gives diners a completely different eating experience by plunging them into pitch darkness to have their meal. By discarding the predominantly used sense of sight, visitors are forced to question their own preconceptions about the whole experience of eating and to re-evaluate the notion of taste and of touch as they are served by blind waiting staff. Whatever the judgement on the food, it is the theatre of the dining experience, which keeps people going back for more.

Another way of injecting theatre is to challenge people's perceptions about what is normal. So water is not colourless, it's white or it's blue. Alcoholic drinks are green. You're playing with your guests' minds and emotions.

Costumes bring a very obvious dash of theatre to an event. Either get guests to arrive in costume or have ready-made outfits ready at the door that they can pull on over their own clothes. The costumes don't have to be complicated, deciding on one colour or texture that all the guests have to wear immediately creates a sense of drama.

Mood-altering techniques
No, not mind-bending hallucinogenic drugs, but easy ways in which a party-giver can control the mood of his or her guests. Theatre has always been about moving people through a series

of emotions, and that's exactly what the best events are all about – orchestrating mood so that guests feel like they've had an experience.

People might think that in a party situation, the only emotion you want people to feel is fun, but unless you contrast that with something else, it's boring. You'd normally contrast it with surprise or shock, but it could be anything. It's the switching between moods that creates the excitement.

Alcohol is our most common means of escape or mood transformation. The second you've had a glass of wine or beer, your perceptions start changing, your mood starts changing. So if it takes one £3 glass of wine to start changing people's moods, you can achieve quite a big change if you start with an alcoholic drink plus something unusual such as touching or colouring the drink. You're not talking big budgets, you're talking about getting it right, understanding your audience, and understanding your role in the whole thing, your goals.

Sound is a very inexpensive way of influencing mood. One of the techniques Theme Traders use is to use contrasting styles of music in different areas. As people come in, there might be one very identifiable style of music playing – Mozart, dance music, jazz, heavy metal or maybe even just a drum beat. That immediately creates a mood, particularly if it's played very loud. Then, if you want to change their mood again, you have completely contrasting style of music playing in the next room.

After a drink and a half you take them into another room, or else just change the style of music a third time. It keeps up a momentum of surprise and influences how they feel. If you combine it with the touch and the alcohol and being taken into different rooms, they're going to feel like they're at an event, rather than just a group drink.

Interaction

Throwing a party is hard work. That may sound obvious, but it's incredible the amount of people who think the purpose of their party is to entertain themselves. Wrong. The guests are not there to provide the entertainment. If you're giving a party it's up to you to make sure your guests have a good time, whether that means doing it yourself or employing someone else to do it for you.

It's vital to make sure everyone is introduced in some way. In corporate events there are badges and table settings, but in private parties, it could be a case of appointing various deputies and charging them with going around making sure people are mingling and no one is left out.

If people are involved in the party, they'll have a good time. If they're standing around on the perimeters feeling a little out on a limb, they might still have a good time, but then again they might not. There's much more margin for feeling isolated.

Try and think of a technique for getting people to interact whether it's just introducing people randomly and giving them a ridiculous conversation starter, "This is X, he's come over to talk to you about sausages/why tiddlywinks should be an Olympic sport". Or playing party games; it's vital to get everyone feeling like they're part of something. Party games are a terrific ice-breaking tool – just think back to Elizabeth Anson and her advocacy of 'sardines' – but it's important to find a way of doing them so that the less extrovert guests don't feel threatened.

"That's a mistake I've seen a number of times," warns David. "If someone is not up for it and you push them into doing it, then it can really bring down the mood of an occasion."

Providing a focal point to the party can immediately bring people together. For example, having a caricaturist in the lobby doing quick sketches of guests as they come in is a great way of getting people talking. Immediately there is an obvious grouping, and an even more obvious conversation starter.

A party-planner's party: Kim

"I love throwing parties. I've had all sorts at the house in Hampstead Garden Suburb. I had an Africa party there and a horror party, complete with hanging vampire in the garden as people walked in. We also had an Arabian Nights party with a Bedouin tent in the garden and Ali Baba greeting guests at the gate. The main thing is the 'Wow Factor'. Give people drinks as they come in, don't be mean, don't let it run out. Have places where people can get together and something for them to talk about. The minute you give someone a drink and a bit of music so they have to shout a bit, they start to have fun. If you go to a party where there's too much space, nothing going on, the music's too low and the white wine is warm, there's nothing to bond you with anyone else."

A party-planner's party: David

"Themed Parties don't have to be big productions. For my last birthday, I took over my local Italian restaurant and turned it from contemporary Italy to period Italy very easily, with a couple of classical statues and some ambient lighting and candles. One of the most important things I did was change the configuration of the seating. The norm now is for small tables, or rounds, but if you make up longs or zigzags, it becomes instantly less easy to place. I invited 30 people and I dressed them all in uniform togas when they came in. Some stripped off completely, others kept their clothes on underneath. The people then became the production. I could have gone mad with stone tablets etc, but I didn't. I had a couple of beautiful living statues around and a harpist as a substitute for a lyre. It really worked. Everyone became part of it, everyone was the same, everyone had something to talk about straight away, something in common. It was great escapism."

5 essential things to remember when throwing a party:

- Make sure the entrance is clearly visible. Make a big sign with the house number on it by the gate, or set up burning flares.
- Never count on guests or friends who offer to help with food or running the bar – inevitably they'll want to be off enjoying the party.
- If guests are likely to dance, decide which area you're going to dedicate as a dance floor and make sure it's safely away from the bar.
- Buy plenty of loo paper, and check the state of the toilets regularly.
- Research reliable local mini cab companies and have the numbers easily to hand and visible.

CHAPTER SIXTEEN
riding the recession

Towards the end of 2009, the dark clouds of recession started to show early signs, if not of dispersing, then at least of shifting slightly. Ironically, it was the top-end, luxury events, which seemed to be coming Theme Traders' way. The big spenders were still around, only now, instead of wanting the rest of the world to know about it, events were more low key and on a more intimate scale. Whereas prior to the crash, parties had been about showing off and ego-stroking, now they were more about a quiet demonstration of prosperity and stability.

Theme Traders had always enjoyed links with the middle eastern royal families, including the Sultan of Brunei and continued to help facilitate events of discreet opulence for their wealthy clients, even if they didn't always run entirely to plan. Becky Handley remembers receiving a panicked, last minute call asking her to help celebrate the 18th birthday of a middle eastern Princess, by organising a troupe of performers dressed as clowns to pay a surprise visit to the Princess's penthouse suite in a 5* London hotel that very same night. They were to go in and sing happy birthday on the stroke of midnight.

Obligingly, she and her hastily-assembled performers turned up at 11.30pm as instructed, only to find the place full of women in pyjamas, as men were strictly forbidden. They were ushered into a small bedroom and told to wait until the Princess was 'available'. So they waited, and they waited... until finally at 1, they were told to go through to the Princess's room and sing. Unfortunately no one had consulted the Princess about it. She was on her mobile phone and clearly had more interest in continuing her conversation than listening to a whole load of strangers with red noses and curly wigs who'd materialised uninvited in her bedroom. As the performers tore through a rousing rendition of Happy Birthday, she turned her back and talked louder, not bothering to turn round when they finished and trooped uncertainly out.

Thanks to their luxury clients and practically-psychic forward planning, Theme Traders was able to weather the economic downturn, even while many of its contemporaries were falling by the wayside. Having seen the writing on the wall for the big-budget, corporate party business as early as July 2007, David and Kim had been quietly diversifying, setting into motion new strategies such as adapting the Cricklewood premises to incorporate a one-stop film and photographic studio.

As the 'noughties' trundled to a close, beleaguered events planners pinned their hopes on the one bright spot in an otherwise bleak landscape of continued recession – the 2012 Olympics, to be staged in London. Undeterred by the still recent memory of the damp squib that had been the millennium, the battered and much-depleted industry once again put its faith in the power of a single event to revitalise and replenish its coffers.

Outside of the Games, however, the recession was proving less of a 100m sprint and more of an endless marathon.

The universities continued to send out thousands of event management graduates every year, many willing to start off working for nothing in an industry which had long since reached saturation point. The glut of newcomers into the business kept overall wage levels low, at a time when the credit crunch, with its legacy of redundancies and repossessions, was still causing a lot of people to question whether parties were really morally or financially justifiable.

Of course, this was far from the first time in history this ethical dilemma had been posed. While there were wars going on and people dying of hunger and earthquakes in Haiti and tens of millions of gallons of oil leaking into the sea in the Gulf of Mexico, was it right to be spending hundreds of thousands on one night of indulgence? When local councils were having to choose between cutting elderly services or school funding, could they possibly justify blowing thousands on one fireworks display or street carnival?

For David it's a no-brainer.

Why you should never get David started about whether events are an unjustifiable expense:

"Do we need events? Yes, I'd say we do need them. Obviously, if you look at Maslow's Hierarchy of Needs – a pyramid which has air and food and sleep at its base, personal fulfilment is a few steps up in the list of priorities, but nevertheless it is there. I think events have a vital function in our lives. A great event will give people an experience which they carry with them in the mental memory box that we all have, for a significant amount of time. It gives them an association with something, a bonding with something for a significant amount of time. If you go into a pub for lunch, it's just a pub lunch, but the sort of stuff we're doing is stuff you don't experience every day. So it has a very important impact on people. Our modern lives are a delicate negotiation of 'should I be doing this or that? am I looking after the planet?'. The fact is, it's all purely on loan while we're here. We're an industry that employs thousands of people – hundreds of thousands of people. I don't think it's valid to say we should stop putting on events because it hurts the planet or its not important or it doesn't contribute. We all need diversion as long as it's sustainable.

At Theme Traders, we have always paid great attention to corporate and social responsibility. We're involved with planting trees, supporting charities and the local community among other things. We understand that you can have fun and care for your social and physical environment – the two are by no means mutually exclusive.

Events management didn't exist in the war, it was superfluous, and if there was another war we'd probably be superfluous again, but right now we have an important role to play. Events are creative – they're art. You might as well ask what significance do Michelangelo's paintings have? Actually they have a huge impact. Art has been respected throughout the centuries for a big variety of reasons and what we do is part of the sociological structure of art. Look at the local festivals, look at the

Up-Helly-Aa in the Shetlands. It's an incredibly important fixture in the local calendar and they look forward to it all year long. It's Dickensian to think people can't have fun, fireworks or parties.

As this book illustrates it is possible to have parties at all budgetary levels if you understand the techniques and principles of how to. The extravagance or otherwise of events might fluctuate according to economic climate, but they remain an integral part of our social needs."

Even so, the recession definitely has had a psychological effect on the party industry. For two years, events had been either cancelled entirely or at least severely curtailed. Though, as the first decade of the millennium limped to a close and the corporate party scene started to pick up again, it was not quite the same as it had been. The financial houses which had been held widely responsible for the crash no longer wanted to show off or appear flashy – parties were more subdued, more restrained and considered.

The other change was the type of event that people were looking for. The mid 2000s had been the era of stylised cool – the Buddha Bar, Shoreditch House – understated chic, with low lighting and modular seating. But, maybe as a reaction to the doom and gloom of the preceding couple of years, the late noughties saw a resurgence of interest in the dramatic and theatrical. Increasingly, Theme Traders was asked to provide live performers, or some sort of interactive element, so that guests – whether at a private party or a product launch – were given a theatrical experience.

How to turn product promotion into live theatre:

Suppose the client is a car manufacturer, launching a new model car to the press. They want everything looked at from a 3D aspect, because that's part of their marketing. The idea TT proposes is for journalists to move through three or four different areas. Each area is a mono-colour with the journalists actually dressed in that colour before they enter the room, so the only thing you will actually pick out before you enter the room will be the faces and any message the client wants to give and then you move from that room to the next room. That's what's called Experiential – it's hard-on theatre but you are involved in it. So you're the one dressed up, you're the one in the pink room with all the the pink stuff.

Theme Traders has always worked on a basis of 2000 events per year. Much less and they risk being underemployed, more and they could be overstretched. That figure hasn't changed throughout the lean recession years, although the type of event and the spend per head has dipped.

Increasingly, Kim and David are looking beyond straight events at other potential areas of expansion like renting out their colourfully eccentric premises – already frequently featured – further afield. Increasingly there are signs that this type of lateral thinking is paying off.

Having already weathered the recession of the early 1990s, Theme Traders has been better placed than some of its rivals to make it through the past few difficult years. Besides, David and Kim aren't related to David Jamilly (the first) for nothing. They grew up with the mantra that you have to adapt to a changing market, and that's exactly what they've done.

The political landscape may have altered recently with the arrival of the new coalition government, but any hopes of a quick end to the credit crunch continue to look like wishful thinking. Still, you know what the old adage says – when things get tough, the tough get partying!

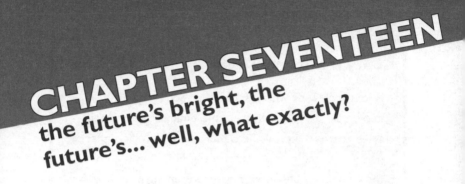

CHAPTER SEVENTEEN
the future's bright, the future's... well, what exactly?

David and Kim are a long way from power freaks but Theme Traders is their baby and, as any proud parent will tell you, it's hard to see your pride and joy being handed over to someone else, no matter how much you admire and trust them.

Over the past few years, they've put measures in place to plan for their eventual retirement – sending key staff on business courses, such as Disney's event and entertainment management course at the Disney Institute in Florida, and appointing deputy directors with the experience and confidence to run the show if either of the bosses aren't around. Training up the next generation of management is a shrewd investment in the future, and yet with the company still so closely wrapped up in Kim and David's personalities, any hand over is going to have to be gentle (think 'allies in post war Berlin' kind of hand-over time frame, rather than a 'grabbing the baton in the 400m relay' time-frame).

One of the big problems is that both of them just enjoy it too much. Neither are the type of people to sit around on matching sofas wearing one of those fleecy blankets with sleeves, marking off telly programmes for the week in the TV guide. Theme Traders is hard work, it's relentless and at times it's downright nerve-racking, but it keeps them constantly questioning, constantly thinking ahead, constantly alive.

Gary Davison on David:

"He is somebody who is focused on achievement. I don't mean achievement for achievement's sake; it's self achievement, the things he wants to do in his life, either personal or business. He's searching. He's always pushing the boundaries of himself, always presenting himself with challenges."

During the worst of the recession, just keeping the company going was enough of a challenge, but now the pressure has died down a bit, they have the time and breathing space to go back to longer-term planning. Their ambition has always been to establish Theme Traders as the benchmark for party planning and prop hire, as synonymous with quality as Harrods or Rolex. "Quality will always endure," says business advisor Maurice the Butcher. "The real asset of Theme Traders is its people – people make it money and people make it a legend."

Already the company is looking to double its current turnover within the next three years. Butcher Maurice favours selling the existing London properties and moving the company to somewhere like Luton, where they could buy 100,000 to 150,000 square feet of industrial space that would combine workshop, storage and depot. Kim and David, born and raised in the Capital and still avid consumers of its cultural riches, will take some persuading.

Much in the same way Kim decided what she needed most in her life was a sabbatical, she often declares she'd be happier in semi-retirement. "I have an innate, inner laziness," declares the woman who regularly works 6 days a week, 16 hours a day. "I'd like to sit in my garden with a bottle of wine and watch the birds."

The trouble is that watching birds can become just a little bit boring (remember the days when the spiders were your friends, Kim?) and Kim is someone who can't abide being bored. David even less so. In every sphere of his life, he's constantly looking for new challenges, which is why when Channel Four asked him to appear on its popular reality TV programme, Secret Millionaire, he accepted, despite knowing it would take him way outside of his comfort zone. The people he met while filming in Redcar last year, and the projects he has supported ever since, have brought a new focus and richness to his life, and he remains actively involved with the town.

But when it comes to his professional life, while he periodically tells himself he should be finding a new mountain to conquer, he comes back up against the almost certain knowledge that few jobs could ever come close to capturing the excitement, diversity, theatre and creativity that Theme Traders gives him. Each day, each phone call, brings the promise of something different. One could be a television company needing to hire a prop for a programme the next night, another might be a drinks company needing a giant beer bottle for a promotional exhibition and the next could be an American billionaire wanting to throw a million pound party in the Caribbean for his wife's birthday party. It's the unpredictability of the business that keeps him and Kim coming into work each morning, long after the financial imperative has eased – that and the buzz of satisfaction when a client calls after an event to say "wow, that was *amazing*".

Plus, as David points out, with the event management industry in a perpetual state of flux, they're learning new things all the time. When the company started out, trying to explain what his job was to a stranger at a party who'd made the mistake of using the "what do you do?" line could take all night. But now it's a respected career choice studied by thousands of undergraduates each year and the subject of numerous academic studies and best-selling books. David and Kim often go and give lectures to businesses and students, and universities send their undergraduates to troop around the Cricklewood empire.

University challenge:

For a duo who left school at fifteen, there's a certain quiet satisfaction in finding themselves regular fixtures on the university guest lecture circuit. David and Kim have established strong links with several universities including Thames Valley, Leeds Metropolitan and Greenwich, as well as places further afield like the University of Technology in Sydney.

With new research into the psychology of events coming out all the time, not to mention new technical innovations, it's an exciting time for the party planning industry, and the Jamillys are always exploring new directions and expanding frontiers. In July 2009, David was a guest speaker at the World Events Summit in Australia, while 2010 saw a lecturing tour in Singapore to be followed by a stint in America in early 2011. For two people who thrive on the shock of the new, the idea of throwing in the towel when there are still so many exciting things to learn would be unthinkable.

So at the moment there are no immediate plans for retirement. Don't forget about David Jamilly and his travelling cinema and Victor and the Laurence Corner emporium – the Jamilly siblings are genetically programmed to spot the gaps in a changing market and put ideas in to action, not to knit socks or play golf.

Maurice the Butcher (long-term business advisor):

"Are Kim and David indispensable? It's a question that concerns them a lot. The strength of their business all the way through has been their personalities and their ability to build confidence in their company. I think they're both very conscious there will come a point where they are able to step back and let good people run the business. It's still a work in progress, but it's underway. Having said that, they might never want to bow out. If they've still got the drive and desire to grow the business and move forward then that's what they'll do."

The original motivation behind Theme Traders – to prove to dad Victor, that they could do very well without him, thank you very much – has long since become obsolete, and yet something still inspires the siblings to keep going, and to keep striving for ever higher standards, ever bolder ambitions. What they've created is more than a business, it's a family. As with all families, there might be fallings out and differences in approach, but when put to the test, they've always got each other's backs.

Gary Davison (childhood friend and music executive):

"David believes that if you sit still, you go backwards. The moment you think you're in a comfortable place is the moment when the car behind you overtakes."

Bernard O'Neill (friend and businessman):

"Whatever happens, the spirit of Theme Traders will remain tied up in David and Kim. They're both eccentric characters who always think outside the box – in fact they've built their own box!"

In many ways, the story of Theme Traders is the story of event management itself – this almost indefinable industry that spans theatre, artistry and corporate hospitality and somehow manages at the same time to fulfil our basic human need for continuity, bonding, belonging, memorable experience and plain fun. The company was born in the same era as the industry it serves, and the two have, in a sense, grown up in tandem, each reflecting and being moulded by the changing sociological and political landscape of the last twenty years.

For Kim and David, Theme Traders also represents a link to the generations of Jamillys that have gone before them – to Granddad David and Father Victor, who also seized on the opportunities presented by the times in which they lived. It's a job, it's a family, it's a link in the chain of history, both general and personal. And every work day is literally a party.

How many other businesses can honestly say that?

"**Change, change, change** is my mantra for business. Remember that just because something worked in the past doesn't mean that it is going to work today or ever again in the future.

Give, give, give is my mantra for living. Strangely enough I've always found that if you follow this you will always have plenty, as one ounce of goodness is worth more than million$ in the bank.

I never set out to make a fortune, I just wanted to try my hardest and do my best.

Whatever you work at and whatever your circumstances, we are all equal and have exactly the same capacity for happiness. Everything we have is on loan in our lifetimes.

It strikes me as strange that the goal for so many people is wealth in the material sense. It was never like that for me, and so I guess it might be thought equally strange that financial rewards have been so forthcoming. Or perhaps that says something in itself.

I count myself lucky to have met some wonderful people in my life.

Too many to recount, but none more deserving of mention than my friends in Redcar, Teesside whom I had the privilege of meeting while making Secret Millionaire and whose selfless example has reaffirmed in me the conviction that giving – whether its time, money or just caring – brings far greater personal rewards than any amount of professional or financial success.

Perhaps this sounds a bit sentimental for a successful businessman, but I truly believe that in life, we must treat others as we would like to be treated, at the same time as being as honest as we can about ourselves. This is the best advice and business formula that I know.

I am especially lucky to have worked for all these years with Kim, my sister, who has always supported me in everything I do and is very much equal in the success of our business and to Michel who has always open-heartedly been a generous friend.

Surrounding myself with positive people who act with integrity has enabled me to rise to new challenges and to have the courage to follow my own path, which is all any of us can do. I don't think there's a set way to become successful, except just to keep learning and keep thinking about how what we do affects other people. I did Secret Millionaire because I wanted to push myself beyond my comfort zone; now I'm taking on a new challenge in founding Kindness Day UK, along with fellow humanitarian Louise Burfitt-Dons. Cynics may scoff, but in a society where the consumer is king, what's wrong with celebrating giving instead of just buying? At the end of the day, we're here for such a short time and we should aim to leave the world a slightly better place than when we found it.

Life is short. Let's party!